HR Futures 2030

HR Futures 2030

A Design for Future-Ready Human Resources

ISABELLE CHAPPUIS AND GABRIELE RIZZO

First published 2022

by Routledge
2 Park Square, Milton Park, Abingdon, Oxon
OX14 4RN

and by Routledge
605 Third Avenue, New York, NY 10158

Routledge is an imprint of the Taylor & Francis Group, an informa business

© 2022 Isabelle Chappuis and Gabriele Rizzo

British Library Cataloguing-in-Publication Data
A catalogue record for this book is available from the British Library

Library of Congress Cataloging-in-Publication Data
A catalog record has been requested for this book

ISBN: 978-1-032-00108-1 (hbk)
ISBN: 978-1-032-00103-6 (pbk)
ISBN: 978-1-003-17279-6 (ebk)

Publisher's Note
This book has been prepared from camera-ready copy provided by the authors.

To Alice, Caroline, and Arnaud,
Isabelle

To Elisabetta, my courageous, curious princess,
Gabriele

May you make the infinite gamut of possibilities yours…
and create your positive futures.
Isabelle and Gabriele

Table of contents

Preface

Now more than ever companies need to be creators of talent, not users of talent.

Rapid technological evolution, changing demographics and shifting workforce expectations are leading us to ramp up the way we work, learn and serve our customers. As a global business-to-business powerhouse, Firmenich is the largest privately-owned fragrance, taste and ingredients leader, delighting thousands of clients who are, in turn, responding to rapidly changing consumer needs.

Creating an agile organization and an ecosystem that puts these changing customer and consumer needs center stage and empowers employees to be aware of critical megatrends is pivotal to be set up for future success.

MIEKE VAN DE CAPELLE
Firmenich
Chief HR Officer

Automation, digitization, and data will significantly impact 30% of our global workforce in the next 5 years, a figure that will only increase over the next decade. For Firmenich, our commitment as a leader in responsible business is to make this impact positive by proactively deploying upskilling initiatives to sustain the capabilities, productivity and retention of our talent.

Every responsible company has an activist role to play in the fight against human obsolescence. Understanding how technology and societal changes will impact skills across a variety of roles in the organization is a difficult but necessary task if we want to adequately prepare our workforce to remain the driving force behind our success.

Foresight thinking is a critical muscle every business leader needs to develop; not tomorrow, today.

I very much applaud the Futures series launched by Isabelle Chappuis and Gabriele Rizzo under the Futures umbrella of HEC Lausanne. Not only do they provide the right case for change, their approach offers a very practical, actionable framework for organizations to assess their gaps and strengths. Foresight thinking is a critical muscle every business leader needs to develop; not tomorrow, today. This HR Futures 2030 is only the beginning of the journey. Many of the new skills are interconnected into a larger universe of capabilities that span functions and organizational processes. This is what makes this work not only pioneering, but truly impactful when accompanied by a clear vision of the future. Are you ready?

We are called to be architects of the future, not its victims.

Richard Buckminster Fuller
Architect, 1895–1983

Foreword

Since 1911, HEC Lausanne has been training future executives and business leaders to become active players in the world of business and economics. Today, we are recognized as one of the top management and economics schools worldwide.

To train forward-looking specialists who are capable of incorporating the perpetual changes in our world into their approach and strategy, HEC Lausanne grows strong in its research community, renowned for the excellence of its work and academic background. We are a wide range of experts, including economists, sociologists, and psychologists, who are among the leading specialists in their fields. We comprise more than 350 bright minds, aiming to understand the fundamental mechanisms of our economic world.

We explored images of possible HR Futures and distilled an elixir of visions for HR leaders, for their consideration, reflection, anticipation, and action.

The Future of Work had to be one of our main axes of thinking. The World of Work as we know it may eventually cease to exist, as the values on which it is based evolve to be no longer relevant or no longer sustainable. We see the change incoming at the horizon, approaching at an unbelievable speed.

The Digital transition is well on its way. The Environmental transition is urgently needed. But neither of them will be successful without a Human transition.

JEAN-PHILIPPE BONARDI
University of Lausanne
Professor of Strategy
Dean of HEC Lausanne

Crises, instability, unpredictability, and at the same time an ever-increasing value rewarding those able to unlock the opportunities past the shocks have even more broadened and intensified the need for change. How to choose what to change? How to advise organizations on the best course to chart to prepare for this wave front of change arriving at an untold velocity?

We should think of all this as a *wake-up call* and *warm-up lap* and prepare for the next deep waves of change that will reshape the labor market and increase demand for future-infused skills. We need to anticipate the incoming disruptions.

At the boundary between the human element and the industrial complex, there lies the prism that those who are developing our leaders of tomorrow must focus on: the HR function.

Vis-à-vis dramatic contextual shocks – as we most likely will be increasingly seeing – HR deliverables of talent, leadership, and support for qualitative growth will become even more *pivotal*.

An anticipatory HR can help make sure that the immediate execution can be safely implemented with peace of heart, while continually anticipating and planning for what's next in an ever-evolving world of work. HR leaders are at the forefront of this Human transition. They can and must support shaping a better world – of work.

HEC Lausanne uses leading-edge research to train competent and responsible executives and entrepreneurs and to advise organizations, businesses, and policymakers – and the international press has awarded us for top-class education and excellent research. We strive to be a real springboard to the future, aiming to prepare our classes to understand the issues associated with the disruptions in our world – to become true visionaries. At the heart of our mission lies this synergy between teaching and research that has ensured HEC Lausanne's success for more than 100 years.

All of this brought us to this volume. Through a bespoke methodology by the foresight unit of HEC Lausanne and the expertise of more than 40 of the best experts our country can offer, we explored images of possible HR Futures and distilled an elixir of visions for HR leaders, for their consideration, reflection, anticipation, and action.

We are preparing all the necessary ground work for another 100 years of successes – yours.

On disruptions and foresight

ISABELLE CHAPPUIS

GABRIELE RIZZO

Today's disruptions are a warm-up lap for future challenges.

The pervasiveness of the digital dimension, the tidal waves in technologies spanning biology, materials science, robotics, physics, chemistry, medicine and post-Convergence disciplines, not to mention the COVID-19 pandemic, are driving a profound metamorphosis of the world.

Feelings of instability, insecurity and disruptions will only increase in the years to come, despite our perspective course towards post-scarcity. The world of work will change and keep changing, adapting, and transforming, sometimes incrementally, sometimes drastically.

How can we plan as early as possible to seize the opportunities coming with these seismic shifts?

We need to understand the future disruption, shroud the veil of complexity, and distill the actions to be envisioned today to keep, or create, the competitive advantage.

This is Foresight.

While foresight has existed for decades, despite its widespread adoption in fields such as Defense and the Oil & Gas industry, little has reached the enclaves of top leadership so far, let alone of education leadership. Foresight should not remain an exercise in style. It should be performed, used and promoted to offer leaders new images of the future upon which they then can act and for which they can prepare to face possible futures and shape their desired ones. This book is shaped around bringing all the majesty of futures specifically to HR leaders.

Foresight does not mean promoting a dystopian view of the world and bringing fear. It aims to bring hope and alternatives for greater growth, wealth, resilience, and abundance.

We lead futures thinking at HEC Lausanne.

We exist to empower individuals, entities and organizations to out-think uncertainty, out-imagine the unknown, and out-vision the status quo for them to own, shape, and design their futures – with a plan.

In this volume we exercise long-term, anticipatory thinking, to illuminate futures linked to the world of work and the place of humans within it.

With this work, we hope to inspire the design of your positive futures.

We exist to empower individuals, entities and organizations to out-think uncertainty, out-imagine the unknown, and out-vision the status quo for them to own, shape, and design their futures – with a plan.

Executive summary

Technology is impressing change onto society at a speed we cannot grasp. Technology grants impressive feats and extraordinary gains: a Maasai Warrior on a mobile phone has better mobile communications than President Reagan did 32 years ago; and, if he were on Google, he would have access to more information than President Clinton did just 20 years ago. In this accelerated and evolving world, fractally multifaceted and in persistent metamorphosis, the dimension of market and business has to chart a new course to keep thriving in complexity, uncertainty, and the unknown. It is not so much a choice as a tenet; since the birth of society, business has been fundamental for it to sustain and grow. Organizations are the capstone here, being the crossroads where work meets economy. The function of HR is the key ambassador in this journey, as the boundary between the human dimension and the industrial complex.

As the sheer reach of the incoming tidal wave of transformation is revealed by the changes we are experiencing today, we need not to consider it as a wave, but as a warm-up instead. To anticipate, understand and channel the forces at work in the impending landscape ten years out, we need to field all our capacity to foresee, and to be prepared for, the unforeseen.

Why a "design"? The scope and complexity of the challenges lying ahead in the world of work demand a different approach than that offered by a classic "strategy". This book aims to frame the problem and present a way forward while acknowledging that there is inherent and fundamental uncertainty in both the problem definition and the proposed solution.

Accordingly, leaders will make their best initial assessment of the environment, formulate a way ahead, and move out. But as they move, they will continually assess the environment to ensure that it responds in a way that is consistent with achieving their goals. Where necessary, they will need to make adjustments, thereby challenging themselves to approach the limits of performance.

A common misconception regarding futures thinking (say 10 years out) is that decisions only exist in 2030. Decisions do not accumulate at the further end of the time horizon.

This Design for Future-Ready Human Resources is a guide for this endeavor. It aims to provide the right lenses through which to focus behaviors and investments, looking out to 2030 but with actionable decision cues in the present. A common misconception regarding futures thinking (say 10 years out) is that decisions only exist in 2030. Decisions do not accumulate at the further end of the time horizon. Some decisions might need to be made today, or in three years' time, to have the desired effect in 10 years. And maybe other factors need attention, or a refocus, to prepare the ground for that decision to be made in three years, both this year and in the years to come. More details about programs, funding, timelines, and industry-specific tailoring are part of a detailed execution of this Design into a Strategy that we try to prepare the reader for in the chapter about Constellations.

We explored a multitude of futures employing state-of-the-art foresight methodologies used in the world of Defense, combined with the expertise of the Authors and HEC Lausanne at the University of Lausanne.

The results are a mythology (keep reading for more details), a selected assessment of Traits of Futures, a detailed description of the disciplines envisioned in a future-ready HR, and an actionable plan to prepare future HR leaders with the skills they need.

A NEW MYTHOLOGY OF THE ORGANIZATION

Our work starts with the definition of five mythological figures – the Demigod, the Centaur, the Knight, the Minotaur and the Monk – to provide metaphors representing the different levels of integration (in their functional, physical, or other meanings) between human and autonomous, intelligent machines. By offering a chance to relate to the appropriate archetype, the Mythology is an atlas to situate oneself in the evolving geography of the HR function and navigate its changes without being in uncharted waters.

10 TRAITS OF FUTURES FOR WORK AND HR

"The" future does not exist: there are infinite possible trajectories from today to 2030, and thus the future comes in many guises, what futurists call "images of the futures". We explored eight possible futures combined in 32 variants to pinpoint the characteristics in them most compelling, urgent, and transversal across the range of futures. These Traits of Futures have a connection to weak signals surfacing in the present, making them relatable and forward-looking at the same time, to provide a strong drive to long-term thinking for the futures of work and HR. The 10 Traits are:

- **More, Faster**: the speed and impact of technology, exerting a change on skills and upskilling, stages of working life, and organizations' processes conducted organically, from recruitment to retirement.

- **Digital's Cleaving Power**: the re-ontologizing might of digital technologies that allows to "cut and paste" meaning in our reality.

- **Community**: the self-organized human response to transitions happening at a very high speed, mediated by cyberspace and technology.

- **Trust**: the intangible enabler for organizations to surf the tidal waves of disruptions through the empowerment of individuals and the technology they are using and developing.

- **Centaurs & Knights**: the new and different ways in which the compression of time brought by exponential technologies forces different generations to integrate the best of human and machine intelligence.

- **Dematerialized Work**: transformational takeaways for new strategic setups of organizations facing taskization, pulverization, and servitization of work and economy.

- **AI & Humans**: the capacity of artificial intelligence and machine cognition to scale individuals up, out, and within.

- **Opportunities**: technology-mediated potentials to overcome boundaries of careers, positions, education, gender preconceptions and the physical presence of individuals and even institutions.

- **Enabling Laws**: the jurisprudence enabling a new enforcement of ethics in data, social security and cyber security, bringing fairer and more equitable access to abundance.

- **New Value Schemes**: the new generation's posture towards business encompasses trust, responsibility, attention, merit, and sustainability as part of the most privileged core assets for companies.

22 DISCIPLINES FOR A 22ND-CENTURY-ORIENTED HR

The Traits of Futures are the main forces to be factored in the equation of the futures. They model, like incorporeal potters, the clay describing the future landscape. Depending on their combination, the resulting "vase" has a different form, fit, and function. In this book, we identify 22 Disciplines, some evolving as bifurcation and recombination of existing HR roles today under the drive of the Traits, others blossoming just in the fertile terrain of the futures. The initial cues for this analysis emerged from more than 350 future ideas and concepts across the range of futures.

As new disciplines will surface, aggregate and develop in uncharted waters of the futures, new HR leaders will need to grow their skills to understand this sea, navigate its waves of change, and make the team thrive in a solid ship.

We designed these disciplines as support for the assessment of organizations' current level of future-readiness, as a potential lever to empower their evolution, and as a guide for HR leaders to prepare and anticipate the change. To support readers towards targeted actions, we also propose visual guidelines towards becoming more future-enabled both for individuals (according to their archetype in the mythology) and for three tiers of organizations (small and medium-sized enterprises (SMEs), Public Administration, and Multinationals).

A PLAN FOR FUTURE HR LEADERS

As new disciplines surface, aggregate and develop in uncharted waters of the futures, new HR leaders will need to grow their skills to understand this sea, navigate its waves of change, and make the team thrive in a solid ship. To undertake this endeavor, we identify four key areas of a learning plan:

- Hard and functional skills: develop business knowledge and leverage technology, being knowledgeable in the traditional "art" of HR but enhancing it with a competence in science, data, and sustainability

- Soft and fusion skills: build, grow and radiate trust for engagement, developing competence to be at the interface of both human and machine cognition, and mastering their blending

- Amplifying and inspirational skills: set the example, respect and gain respect for effective impact, leading from above and from within

- Transformative and evolution skills: lead culture and knowledge development for sustained change, integrating what drives the current and the emerging workforce into a single, holistic narrative.

Although this study has no claim of exhaustiveness, we trust that – through thorough research of human, collective, fictional and artificial intelligence, and having brought brilliant minds and ideas together during our foresight event – we have shed some new light on the HR function. This volume aims to be both a wake-up call and a toolbox for HR leaders, to enable them to anticipate the future and prevent a "strategic shock" in a future unfolding to shape their world without them having a plan.

While some of the concepts found in this volume may seem already known or even mainstream to some, they may be perceived from others as totally futuristic and unorthodox or detached from reality. We hope, however, that through the visions, designs, and guidelines in this book, all our readers will be able to bridge the chasm that is separating their potential from their agency.

This volume aims to be both a wake-up call and a toolbox for HR leaders, to enable them to anticipate the future and prevent a "strategic shock" in a future unfolding and to shape their world without them having a plan.

INTRODUCTION

Context

For as long as humanity can recall, business has allowed society's growth and sustainment to its continuation. Business organizations exist as part of a society, and in its very interest.[1]

Yet the last centuries' purpose of business organizations has been distorted to suit the 20th-century conception of capitalism. Our current economic system, based on private ownership of the means of production and their operation for profit, has been considered the utmost optimal solution until society realized that we came at a crossroads with massive social fissures.[2]

We are living in an era of massive shifts in ethical consciousness, with an increased need to rewrite the very concept of our economy.[3] A rethink of what a business organization is fundamentally about might be necessary to meet the challenges posed by the demands of the stakeholder of tomorrow. As it might be the time to revisit the very nature of the business organization, some call for a great reset,[4] which should not be channeled within established theories, but along the grand plan of humanity's long-term goals and how to achieve them.

A new mindset is needed to be fit for facing this century's complex systemic challenges.[5]

Today's pressure on business organizations to pursue the moral high ground is increasing, and we now see the rise of ubiquitous tension between a sustainable, ethical human society and the economic practices of self-regulating markets à la Milton Friedman.[6]

Organizations, entities, individuals, employees and employers have been exposed to these significant changes over the last decades, with special relevance in the world of work. These have been generally driven by the rise of technology and increase in globalization, the financial and economic crisis, and as well the shifting social values along with new sociotechnical paradigms shaping economic and institutional dynamics. Many of these developments have brought unprecedented opportunities, economic growth, and reduced the drudgery of work. However, both surveys around the world and horizon scanning confirm that these rapid changes are driving profound transformations, leaving employers, employees and every stakeholder across the range increasingly anxious and worried about the Future of Work, the mounting human obsolescence, and generally about the future. The world of work is inextricably linked to organizations and their value and role in society; the very notion of work and employment is being shaken, and today the world of work is undergoing significant and fundamental shifts.

In addition to being disrupted by major societal changes, the world of work is also being affected by a major rise in technology progress, literally re-ontologizing our world.[7] With the exponential acceleration of technologies, the convergence of megatrends and the resulting exponential compression of time,[8] the world has gone from complicated to complex, leaving employers and employees without landmarks about where to go next, without control over the world as it was in their comfort zone, and without time to understand, plan and subsequently adapt to this *new normal*.

In such a volatile, uncertain, and ambiguous landscape, the reptilian answer about the Future of Work is fear, anxiety, and concern. In 2013, Oxford professor Carl Frey announced that 47% of all jobs could potentially be automated. By 2020, the trend towards job disruption shows no sign of weakening, and the skill sets needed to be relevant in the labor market are not the same anymore. Jobs are changing and the lifespan of skills is decreasing drastically. War for talents is at record high, with 54% of companies of any size reporting talent shortages.[9] Even in Defense, an environment usually far from being disrupted, the risk of robotization is steadily more than 30%, with peaks of 49%.[10]

In a society where work is a pillar of individual fulfillment and social organization, we believe that the current disruption of the working landscape and the resulting *Human Skills Obsolescence* represents a severe national security threat, which has to be addressed by companies, educational institutions, governments and individuals alike. Indeed, failure to anticipate and plan will lead to a risk increase and will compromise growth and stability. A failure to anticipate education, qualification and skills requirements will endanger the sustainable development of business and cause a massive waste of human, social and financial capital. Upskilling is on track to become the most pressing societal challenge for the next 100 years.[11]

There is no one-size-fits-all solution to (re-)skill individuals, as the "Future of Work" is eminently local. Each country (or even county) has its own educational system, values, and dominating industry, each company its own organization and culture.

The function of Human Resources is the principal ambassador, the nexus, in this journey.

Born in the early 1900, the "HR function's overall purpose is to ensure that the organization is able to 'achieve success' through people".[12] Initially considered as a super-administrator providing services that produce more efficient organizations, HR leaders have increasingly gained in strategic importance and their own *Value Proposition* has evolved, encompassing five main areas[13]:

• Knowing the external business realities (technology, economics, globalization, demographics)

• Serving external and internal stakeholders (customers, investors, stakeholders, employees)

• Creating HR practices (people, performance, information, work)

• Building HR resources (HR strategy and organization)

• Ensuring HR professionalism (HR roles, competencies, development)

Today HR leaders find themselves at the center of a perfect storm, managing a "human capital" that is growingly out of step with its exponentially evolving and demanding environment. They can decide to endure those major mutations or to shape them. This is a unique opportunity for the HR function to grow, evolve and showcase its pivotal and strategic importance as a cornerstone of organizations in this era of great transition.

This foresight initiative is aimed at illuminating futures of the world of work and proposing possible, concrete, actionable new disciplines composing the HR function in the years to come. It intends to help HR leaders set their compass right to anticipate needs, reskill, upskill, and be ready to navigate the arduous waters of the Future of Work.

The potential for identifying futures of a corporate function can only be mobilized through the diversity of perspectives and skills of the various partners involved. It is therefore by bringing together the knowledge available both in our institution and beyond, with the expertise available in our economic ecosystem, that we were able to channel the cues on the future into a design of a future-informed HR function, not afraid to look at the 22nd century.

Welcome to HR Futures 2030.

1   Ahmed, P.K. & Machold, S. (2004). The quality and ethics connection: Toward virtuous organizations. *Journal of Total Quality Management*, 15(4), 527–545.
    Griseri, P. (2013). *An introduction to the philosophy of management.* Thousand Oaks: Sage.
    Platts, M.J. (1997). Greeds' OK, actually. 2nd International symposium on Catholic Social Thought and Management Education. Antwerp.
    Goldman, G.A., Nienaber, H. & Pretorius, M. (A). The essence of the contemporary business organization: A critical reflection. *Journal of Global Business and Technology*, 11, 1–13
2   Gurdus, L. (2018). *Paul Tudor Jones: The $19 trillion private sector should lead social change.* CNBC.
3   Bolton, S.C. & Laaser, K. (2013).
    Work, employment and society through the lens of moral economy. *Work, Employment & Society*, 27, 508–525.
4   Florida, R. (2010). *The great reset: How new ways of living and working drive post-crash prosperity.* Harper.
5   Ross, F. (2020). Kate Raworth – Doughnut economics: Seven ways to think like a 21st-century economist (2017). *Regional and Business Studies*, 11.
6   Bolton, S.C. & Laaser, K. (2013). *Ibid.*
7   Floridi, L. (2013). *The ethics of information.* OUP Oxford.
8   Rizzo, G. (2019). Disruptive technologies in military affairs. In F. Rugge (Ed.), *The global race for technological superiority.* Washington, DC: ISPI and Brookings Institution.
9   Manpower. (2020). *Closing the skills gap: Know what workers want.* ManpowerGroup Survey.
10 *Work in progress.* (2019). HEC Lausanne, University of Lausanne.
11 Probst, L. & Scharff, C. (2019). A strategist's guide to upskilling. *Strategy+Business.*
12 Armstrong, M. (2009). *Armstrong's handbook of human resource management practice.* (11th ed.). London: Kogan Page.
13 Ulrich, D. & Brockbank, W. (2005). *The HR value proposition.* Cambridge, MA: Harvard Business Press.

CO-CREATORS

Designers
& dreamers

Christophe Barman
Loyco
Founder

Isabelle Chappuis
UNIL | HEC Lausanne | Futures Lab
Executive Director

Christine Choirat
Swiss Data Science Center
EPFL & ETHZ
Chief Innovation Officer

Konstantinos Dardougias
Firmenich
Human Resources Specialist

Yves Epiney
Direction Plus SA
Associate Partner

Miral Hamani
Hewlett Packard Enterprise
Director & Associate

Laure Hauswirth
City of Morges
Head of HR Department

Julien Hautle
Swisscom (Suisse) SA
Future Workforce Manager

Bettina Hummer
UNIL | School of Law
Professor

Elodie Jantet
UNIL | Centre de soutien
à l'enseignement
Film Maker

Mahwesh Khan
IMD Business School
Boards & Leadership Researcher

Jean-François Knebel
CHUV
Senior Scientist

Judith Konermann
Philip Morris International
*Global Head of Strategic Workforce
Planning*

Quentin Ladetto
armasuisse S+T
Foresight & Research Director

Rafael Lalive
UNIL | HEC Lausanne
Professor & Vice-Dean

Karine Lammle
Tetra Pak
*Head of HR Country Services
Switzerland*

Bertrand Lanxade
Mazars
Head of Human Resources

Barbara Lax
Little Green House SA
Founding Director

Charlotte Mazel-Cabasse
UNIL-EPFL Digital Humanities Center
Executive Director

Benjamin Mueller
UNIL | HEC Lausanne
Associate Professor

Martial Pasquier
UNIL
*Vice-Rector Human Resources
& Finance*

Gabriele Rizzo
Principal Futurist Advisor for NATO,
U.S. Space Force, U.S. Air Force,
and Italian MoD

Frédéric Roger
AIR HR Global Solutions
CEO & Founder

Muriel Rubin
UNIL | HEC Lausanne | Futures Lab
Head of Strategic Developments

Jérôme Rudaz
HR Vaud
President

Alain Salamin
UNIL | HEC Lausanne
Lecturer

Daniel Samaan
International Labour Organization
Senior Economist

Emmanuel Sylvestre
UNIL I Centre de soutien
à l'enseignement
Director

Ben Thancanamootoo
Co-facilitator
Rapporteur

Jeff Van de Poël
UNIL | Centre de soutien
à l'enseignement
*Head of Digital & Multimedia
Operations*

David Vernez
Center for Primary Care
& Public Health (Unisanté)
Head of Department

Olivier Verscheure
Swiss Data Science Center
EPFL & ETHZ
Director

Tara Yip
Swissquote Bank
Head of Human Resources

Giorgio Zanetti
UNIL
*Vice-Rector Teaching
& Students Affairs*

Guy Zehnder
Firmenich
Director of HR World Operations

Sponsors

HEC LAUSANNE UNIVERSITY OF LAUSANNE

For more than a century, HEC Lausanne has been training future executives and leaders to become active players in the world of business and economics, providing them with solid foundations for their successes, careers and positive futures. As a university-based business school, HEC Lausanne has two main and complementary duties to the community: Research and Teaching.

Its research drives theory and influences practice. The Faculty uses it to train students to be capable, responsible economic leaders and entrepreneurs and to provide sound advice to organizations and policymakers.

As a Swiss public and cantonal institution, HEC Lausanne provides local students and professionals with the knowledge and skills they need to play a leading role in today's globalized economy. It also trains a considerable number of talented students and professionals from abroad, predominantly from Europe, thereby sustaining Switzerland's and Canton of Vaud's long-standing tradition as a knowledge center of international influence and reputation.

HEC Lausanne aims to be recognized locally and internationally as a leading public provider of business education, integrating research-based teaching, high-impact research, and career-conducive curricula.

FIRMENICH

Firmenich is the world's largest privately-owned perfume and taste company, founded in Geneva, Switzerland, in 1895. Driven by its purpose to create positive emotions to enhance well-being, naturally, Firmenich has designed many of the world's best-known perfumes and tastes, bringing delight to over four billion consumers every day for 125 years. Renowned for its world-class research and creativity, as well as its leadership in sustainability, each year, Firmenich invests 10% of its turnover in R&D to understand and share the best that nature has to offer responsibly. Counting 10,000 colleagues across more than 100 markets, Firmenich champions a diverse and inclusive culture that embraces new ways of working for all to thrive.

HR VAUD

Created in 1958, HR Vaud is a non-profit association serving Human Resources professionals representing companies and organizations of all sizes and from all sectors, public or private, local and international. With nearly 900 members, HR Vaud anticipates, supports and promotes the trades linked to human resources and intends to be a force for proposals to economic and political powers.

METHODOLOGY

HR Futures 2030 in 6 Steps

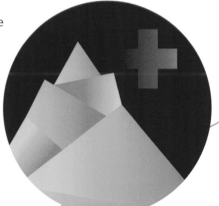

2 Scope all-round futures from technological cases using Future of Work scenarios based on the potential impact of disruptive technologies. Amplify and enrich the scenarios with socio-technical system analysis.

1 Based on the fundamental research needs identified by academia and in collaboration with sponsors, define the desired outcome. Review literature. Run local surveys. Identify, motivate and involve experts and key actors. Design and run the tailor-made foresight methodology.

3 Imagine potential futures for Switzerland, enriching the initial scenarios with Swiss perspectives, encompassing the economic, environmental, societal, security and political fields.

4 Design a future HR function managing workforces in those potential futures and leading to the description of 22 new Disciplines for HR in 2030.

5 Profile the future HR Leader in terms of ideal work style and values, skills and knowledge, experience, and academic and educational credentials.

6 Research supporting evidence of the images of the future designed by the group. Extract the main Traits of Futures relevant for HR, and design new disciplines for a smooth transition towards new organizational identities. Evaluate costs, impact, availability, and readiness. Draft, edit, and design the final output.

Why a foresight for HR

The Authors have developed a unique approach to identify and shape the future of work, its disciplines and skills, harnessing foresight methodologies brought from the world of Defense and applying it to the world of work.

"Foresight" has been around for more than 50 years and, although constantly evolving by nature, it is a very mature "science". Foresight has been extensively developed in Defense since World War II and has been used to anticipate risks and dilemmas linked with national security in general.

Foresight is successfully applied to technology (technology foresight) and strategy (strategic foresight) by defense organizations and companies to maintain a competitive advantage in their field and prevalence in the market. Rarely has it been applied to the definition of work and the education domain or to the purpose of anticipating new skills. This is what was done in this undertaking.

Today, with organizations becoming more blended and adaptive, with the changing landscape of the world of work, with the increasing skills gap and skills mismatch affecting the smooth run of the economy, "human skills obsolescence" is transforming into a potential "national security threat", hence the pertinence of exploiting foresight to tackle this rising problem and remain ahead of the curve, both for organizations and for nations.

The future does not exist per se, there are multiple versions of it that have yet to materialize through our decisions and actions, and it is for us to define its trajectory and identify the skills that will be needed to reach the desired outcome.

The future is ours to shape, which is why besides using new technologies such as AI to scrape the web for weak signals about the future, we use human intelligence and creativity in a collaborative and co-creating setting to design the ideal human profile that will help us evolve towards a positive society.

> *Education is our first line of defense.*
>
> Harry S. Truman, 33rd President of the United States, 1884–1972

MYTHOLOGY

Mythology
of your organization

WHY A "MYTHOLOGY"?

We stand on the brink of a technological revolution that will fundamentally alter the way we live, work, and relate to one another. In its scale, scope, and complexity, the transformation will be unlike anything humankind has experienced before. Technology is undoubtedly the mightiest force when it comes to innovation and the modification of the current landscape. Technology is a powerful exponential thread intertwined with the broader evolutionary forces of our scenario – the enabling woof of the innovation warp in the developing fabric of future univocal advantages. Technology grants impressive feats and extraordinary gains: a Maasai Warrior on a mobile phone has better mobile communications than President Reagan did 32 years ago; and, if he were on Google, he would have access to more information than President Clinton did just 20 years ago.[14] Technological change is on a strong exponential track, with a consistent record over the last few decades.[15] During the last 20 years especially, we have witnessed a technological acceleration unlike anything the world has ever seen. Exponential progress has occurred in artificial intelligence, robotics, infinite computing, ubiquitous broadband networks, digital manufacturing, nanomaterials, synthetic biology, just to name a few. If this becomes a foundational characteristic of this era and this century in particular, contrary to the "common sense" intuitive linear growth, we will not experience 100 years of progress in the 21st century – it will be more like 20,000 years of progress.[16]

It is then manifest that the extraordinary and unprecedented incoming shifts are of a sort resembling those involving supernatural beings or forces that we find for instance in lore, stories, or legends of Ancient Greece.

14   Diamandis, P.H. & Kotler, S. (2012). *Abundance – The future is better than you think*. New York, NY: Free Press.

15   Rizzo, G. (2019). Disruptive technologies in military affairs. In F. Rugge (Ed.), *The global race for technological superiority*. Washington, DC: ISPI and Brookings Institution.

16   Kurzweil, R. (2001). *The law of accelerating returns*. Kurzweil Essays.

17   Dante Alighieri's Divine Comedy – *Paradiso*, Canto XXXIII, lines 112–120.

18   "The limits of my language are the limits of my mind. All I know is what I have words for". Wittgenstein, L. (1921). Tractatus Logico Philosophicus.

19   We picked the Phylum of Chordata, broadly speaking animals with a dorsal nerve cord that are bilaterally symmetric.

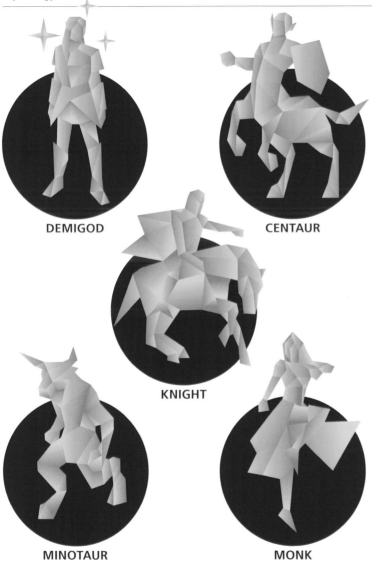

DEMIGOD

CENTAUR

KNIGHT

MINOTAUR

MONK

If we were able to provide an analytical description and a data-driven assessment of the aforementioned shifts, they would not be part of images of the futures ten years from now: they would rather be within the grasp of a time span comparable to the one we use to take note of our schedule, appointments, events and vacations – namely our "Outlook future". We cannot, thus, propose a "design", or a "roadmap", or even less a "plan": we need a tool which embodies and provides an explanation, through descriptive imagery, of phenomena currently transcending the sensemaking capacity of humans. Like Dante describing God Himself in his Paradiso,[17] we need metaphors to provide clarity and identify hidden similarities. We are proposing this "mythology" to offer metaphors for the transition at the horizon, striving to overcome the Wittgensteinian[18] limits of language, and with them the limits of the mind.

In this frame, the meteoric rise of artificial intelligence and machine cognition is the new, modifying force. As there are culturally too many dystopian remnants when giving agency to metaphors cleaving together different categories (e.g. non-living and living), we aimed at using the human together with different representatives within a reasonable set of living creatures,[19] that called upon our imagination of magical combinations. In the mythological figures described below, the AI or more in general the "machine" part is the one from this set, usually bringing powerful traits to the human – but sometimes not without consequences.

Demigod

HUMAN LIVES AI

A Demigod in classical mythology is the offspring of a god and a human, who retains part of the god-like powers perfectly encapsulated in a human-like shape. In our mythology, the divine part is the metaphor for AI, granting inhuman powers (strength, magic, and so on in the classics; access, information, data, and knowledge in this one of ours) but perfectly integrated in a human shape. In this sense, it is more than imagining human "and" AI. The Demigod is a representation of a human that "lives" AI. And it is indeed an existential integration: a Demigod is not one anymore without his powers. These are the most knowledgeable and integrated individuals you can find in your ranks when it comes to both their technology and people parts, open to novelty and experimentation in the first person, abstracting things and ideas, often redefining the problem definition. Their perfect integration with their "artificial DNA" allows them to expand their horizons whenever they feel their current "machine" part limiting them, in any way they find it suitable: improving, changing, even tinkering with it. Unconventional, energetic, and catalyst Demigods retain only superficial similarities with humans, lacking the sensitivity for issues that they can disregard thanks to their "divine" nature.

Centaur

HUMAN AND AI

Inspired by the mythical Greek creature half-horse, half-man, this Centaur is a man-machine *unicum* mixing biological and artificial intelligence into an inextricably linked, converged whole, which is more capable than the sum of its parts alone. The human half brings the brain and the heart to the Centaur, while the machine half provides its strength, speed, and power. Both parts are inseparable, and empower reciprocally, with the human touch as a unique differentiator to raw machine power. This being is not as integrated and free as the Demigod to change, evolve, and modify; there is no way to separate the animal half from the human half. This is the first hint of a being less converged; the other one being the "deformity" of its lower half. For this reason, the Centaur represents human "and" AI: there are higher levels of mutual understanding, and the machine knows what its human counterparts need and vice versa. It is thus a perfect integration of function, but not of form. In this sense, it has fewer "powers" than a Demigod and less grasp of full, overwhelming potential. Conversely, it is more understanding for human issues, by which it is touched on some occasions.

Knight

HUMAN ON THE AI

Extensively trained, refined masters of the art of the sword, diehard (wo)men-at-arms in the collective image of the medieval age and fantasy, the Knight in this mythology is the élite tier of what humans can achieve while still being one with themselves and not extending their identity to autonomous and intelligent systems. Knights represent humans "on" the AI. The Knight lacks the integration and fusion of the Centaur and the identification of the Demigod, and thus does not reach the heights in speed, strength, stamina, resolve and synchronization the other two can. However, the Knight can do what the others cannot: exist without their machine counterpart. The Knight can dismount and act separately from their horse – fight, negotiate, plan, connect, sleep. Their thought process is not dependent on their animal (machine) counterpart. It is true that a vast part of the Knight's training is about equine handling and direction, and the best exploitation of the animal while maneuvering in combat-like high-intensity situations, and so in this sense the Knight's thinking is largely influence by this; however, their direction-setting and decision-making sits on a higher level. Not "being one" with their horse, the Knight can also change horses to find one more suitable to their style, or, whenever the horse is injured or killed, the Knight can still stand his ground independently. True, what is perfect in the matching and connection with the machine for the Demigod is far less seamless for the Knight. What is natural to a Centaur is the result of extensive training for the Knight. Conversely, though, what is natural to the Knight – independence and resilience – is something the Demigod has to plan for, and the Centaur must train (extensively) for. More than just adding the perk of resilience to its picture, the Knight captures something the Centaur cannot: the power of experimentation and of non-dependence from its AI counterpart.

Minotaur

AI ON THE HUMAN

Giovanni Boccaccio writes of the Minotaur in his literary commentary of the Dante's *Commedia* addressing it with superlatives like "most ferocious" and "of astonishing strength".[20] The feralness exuding from this description is the expression of the beastlike part taking over the consciousness, agency, and overall cognitive economy[21] of this converged being. Our Minotaur is clearly devoid of the violent hue accompanying Boccaccio's description while preserving important meta-traits. In the Minotaur, it is the machine part in the lead. It is not an integration, as much as a coercion of function, with form following. The Minotaur in this Mythology might appear instinctive and somewhat erratic to a human eye; it is because AI acts and adjusts at a completely different speed, without the ability to ingest complexity that is unique to the human brain. The incredible strength and determination are a straight consequence of this "upside down" convergence, that while moving the human part at a distance, grants unfiltered access to raw machine speed and power. Minotaurs represent "AI on the human". The human part provides feedback to AI direction, and not the opposite: the human half brings the senses and common sense to the AI. The Minotaur could be fairer and more equitable, provided that the machine part in its autonomy and intelligence follows principles of ethically aligned design,[22] as any sufficiently advanced act of benevolence is indistinguishable from malevolence.[23] Distant from human empathy and with little ability and desire to experiment, the Minotaur has instead great attention to detail and can work extensively on implementation of tasks and details, tuning systems and bringing focus to concepts, and fitting evidence into current systems and structures.

Monk

AI OUT OF THE HUMAN

Despite the Greek etymology meaning "single, solitary", the Monk in this mythology is not a hermit or a neo-Luddite. Instead, in the same way modern monks such as the Shaolin monks train[24] for purity of body and mind – developing impressive physical and inner strength, resistance, and mindfulness –, this Monk is a keen, refined, profound cognoscente of human nature and performance, and a living example of it. A Monk finds wholeness in keeping interaction with the machine at a distance, up to making a point in not interacting with it. Their extraordinary focus on human ability can be a great resource to Knights and Centaurs, who despite a different perception of the world, can find great insight in the Monk's sensemaking, potentially allowing them an evolutionary path. The Monk's full perception of human nature poses them physiologically distant from the issues brought about the "machine" half, and with a hard time understanding the Centaurs' and Demigods' world.

20   "[...] una creatura la quale era mezza uomo e mezza toro. Il qual cresciuto, e divenuto ferocissimo animale e di maravigliosa forza, dicono che Minos il fece rinchiudere in una prigione chiamata «laberinto»". Boccaccio, G. *Il Comento alla Divina Commedia e gli altri Scritti intorno a Dante*. Curated by Guerri, D. (1918). Laterza, Italy, p. 312.

21   Bayne, T. (2008). The phenomenology of agency. *Philosophy Compass*, 3(1), 182–202.

22   The IEEE Global Initiative on Ethics of Autonomous and Intelligent Systems. (2018). *Ethically aligned design: A vision for prioritizing human well-being with autonomous and intelligent systems* (1ˢᵗ ed.). See also IEEE P7000™ Standards Working Groups.

23   Rubin, C.T. (1996). First contact: Copernican moment or nine day's wonder? In S.A. Kingsley & G.A. Lemarchand (Eds.), *The search for extraterrestrial intelligence (SETI) in the optical spectrum II* (p. 168). Bellingham, WA: The International Society for Optical Engineering.

24   Martial arts training is not mandatory in the Shaolin Monastery.

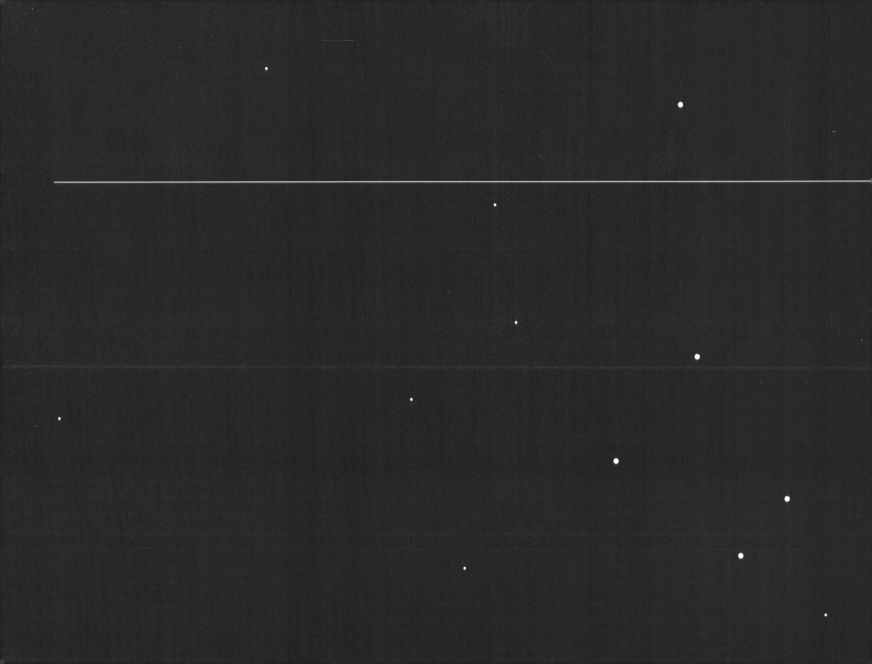

TRAITS OF FUTURES

The problems of the world cannot possibly be solved by skeptics or cynics whose horizons are limited by the obvious realities. We need men who can dream of things that never were and ask 'why not?'

John F. Kennedy, 35th President of the United States (1917–1963)

10 Traits of Futures

The 10 Traits of Futures are a collection of characteristics that we believe 2030 will have. Their weak signals surface in the present time, and in fact emerged from the brainstorming sessions centered on several plausible futures. These signals were identified, highlighted, amplified and described earlier during Step 6.

The list is obviously non-exhaustive. However, we find these 10 traits to be the main ones most relevant for the HR function in 2030, and at the source of the emergence of new HR disciplines, which are described in the next chapter.

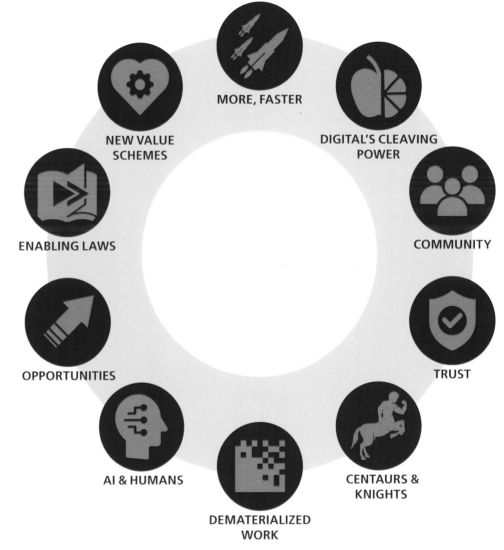

NEW VALUE SCHEMES

MORE, FASTER

DIGITAL'S CLEAVING POWER

COMMUNITY

ENABLING LAWS

TRUST

OPPORTUNITIES

CENTAURS & KNIGHTS

AI & HUMANS

DEMATERIALIZED WORK

1. More, Faster

Over the last two decades, the speed and impact of information technologies have changed every landscape in deep, radical ways. Every two days during 2010, we created as much information as we did from the dawn of humankind up until 2003.[26] In 2017 we have crossed the line to enter the Zettabyte Era[27]: more data were created in that year than in the previous 10,000 years of civilization. The type of data created is expanding rapidly across a wide range of industries: biotech, energy, healthcare, automotive, space and deep-sea explorations, cybersecurity, social media, telecom, consumer electronics, manufacturing, gaming and entertainment – and the list goes on. Underpinned by 2030, access paradigms like 6G are able to provide the technology stratum to carry our five senses across the globe and out to the stars. New converged architectures for privacy and security, new and improved access to data and information, as well as the immense number of devices around the globe topping 1 trillion,[28] the sheer volume of data in 2030 will hardly be commensurable by any human mean. With Data Lakes widely flooded, the paradigm will move towards "Data Oceans".[29] More data, more bandwidth, more access, and more transparency will provide access to more knowledge at our fingertips, but with tightly compressed timescales to be able to acquire it. High-value upskilling loops in 2030 will not just be about more content, but chiefly about faster times to go through them with success (not just profit). More knowledge, less time to acquire it, and more pressure to be on the edge will be factors pushing new professional profiles oriented at anticipating and executing several steps of learning and development as much in advance as possible. Conversely, due to the dramatically increased surface of knowledge mastery necessary to remain relevant as a generalist, a strong drive towards uber-specialization will take place especially in the less privileged working environments. With more specialization called upon in faster cycles, and the transformative support of more, faster technology, we will assist a flourish of jobs and platforms born from the servitization of the economy[30] and the "taskization" of certain classes of profiles, namely the tech-enabled pulverization of higher-level profiles into tasks.[31]

"Pulverization" is the unbundling of jobs and profiles in simple and disconnected tasks and skills. "Taskization" is the re-building of different new profiles unimaginable before, giving rise to new jobs. "Servitization" is the globalization of the target market, available offer, and value-added services on a worldwide platform.

On the other hand, wealthier profiles will be able to cope with this faster and more challenging panorama with simply more brainpower, through augmentation or integration with autonomous or intelligent systems as companions. Due to the accelerated rate of lifecycle of skills, obsolescence will be a shock to be experienced many times over one's life – dismantling the idea of a three-stage-life (study–work–retire). These psychological shocks will be plentiful, and closer, due to more job uncertainty, more workload, and faster work cycle from taskization, resulting overall in more job transitions.

The pervasive presence of autonomous, intelligent, even neural technology will enable a knowledge and skill version of the quantified self,[32] resulting in a quantified "learning" self that is able to support and anticipate the upskilling and reskilling of individuals, adaptively, bringing of the paradigm of predictive

human maintenance into realization. For those who will buy into this process, the upside might be seismic. Through the quantified learning self, obsolescence shocks might be mitigated well in advance by putting in action gradual, constant and painless knowledge-skill "upgrades" guided through predictive, personal obsolescence-contrasting algorithms. Conversely, all the effort put into maintaining high employability, continuous learning, and an attractive education, learning and development portfolio, will make individuals more exacting in terms of remuneration and gratification.

More data, more bandwidth, more access, and more transparency will provide access to more knowledge at our fingertips, but with tightly compressed timescales to be able to acquire it.

The global dimension and total interconnectedness of the labor market will push companies to provide quick to immediate gratification through holistic, and even gamified, types of remunerations. Other in-kind types of benefits might be offering a tailored access to more, specific high-value or fast-track learning and upskilling, or dedicated attention to the individual's skill segmentation for more, faster, better improvement and learning tracks. Worldwide competition on the labor market will also call for faster response times in recruitment, leading to improvements on its process and technologies employed. Gamification, virtual reality (VR), and de-humanization of recruitment, in the sense of mediating every exchange through virtual Avatars of human interlocutors will not only bring faster, instant access to a hugely broader talent pool, but will also open new market niches from fashion, to virtual architecture, to platforms. HR functions will be faced with such a degree of speed, complexity and volatility that "old-school" processes will not work anymore. The function, as well as its processes, will have to be re-conceptualized and re-engineered to be effective with a broad range of stakeholders, either in person, remote or even virtual; AI-augmented, neuro-linked, or "purely" human.

26   Siegler, M. G. (2010, 5 August). Eric Schmidt: Every 2 days we create as much information as we did up to 2003. *Techcrunch*.

27   Cisco Blogs. (2016, 9 September). *The zettabyte era officially begins (how much is that?)*.

28   Sparks, P. (2017). *The route to a trillion devices. The outlook for IoT investment to 2035*. ARM White Paper.

29   Artin, C. (2016, 8 July). When data lakes become data oceans, approximation will rise. *IoT Revolution*.

30   This is the phenomenon of hiring independent contractors or freelancers instead of employees, based on flexible, temporary, or freelance jobs, often involving connecting with clients or customers through an online platform offering a service – thus the "servitization". It is the paradigm also known as "Gig economy".

31   We explore the "three -zations" in more detail in *Dematerialized Work*, p. 64.

32   The cultural phenomenon of self-tracking with technology opening the possibility of "self-knowledge through numbers". See Ferris, T. (2013, 3 April). *The first-ever quantified self notes*. https://tim.blog/2013/04/03/the-first-ever-quantified-self-notes-plus-lsd-as-cognitive-enhancer/.

2. Digital's Cleaving Power

The digital "cuts and pastes" reality, in the sense that it couples, decouples, or recouples features of the world, and consequently our assumptions about them, which we always assumed as monolithic and indivisible.[33] It acts by splitting apart and re-fusing in new ways the "atoms" of our experience and culture. Two examples convey the idea clearly. The first example concerns location and presence, and their decoupling. In a digital world, it is obvious that one may be physically located in one place, like at a bus stop, and interactively present in another, like on Twitter or LinkedIn. Yet, all past generations that lived in an exquisitely analogue world conceived and experienced location and presence as two inseparable sides of the same human condition: being situated in space and time, here and now. Action at a distance and telepresence belonged to magic or science fiction. Today, this decoupling simply reflects ordinary experience in any information society. We are the first generation for which "where are you?" is not a merely rhetorical question. The second example is about re-coupling: the blurring and merging of the role of producers and consumers.[34] The highly saturated marketplace and mass production of standardized products brought to a process of mass customization, and thus an increasing involvement of consumers as producers of their own customized products – the consumption of information produced by the same population of producers,[35] for instance.

We are the first generation for which
"where are you?" is not a merely rhetorical question.

The Digital will operate at least three fundamental "cuts and pastes" in the world of labor in 2030.

First, technologies will cleave identity from corporeality. With widespread availability and improvement in bandwidth of several orders of magnitude, the consequent implementation of a deeply integrated digital infrastructure will be straightforward. The circumstances that until now are conceived as entangled with a physical presence will be relaxed, and most of them will be thought of as experienceable in a virtual setting. Through this enabler, and under increased peer pressure and faster market cycles, organizations will either transform their processes to make room for this gargantuan shift in the approach to "presence", or undergo a fragmentary metamorphosis through the revolution of working-level praxes within the organization. The prestige and renown of firms, organizations and companies will be weighted by the branding and the "cool factor" of their digital infrastructure, too. With the advent of extensive VR, identity and corporeality will be cleaved to adhere in the new concept of "virtual existence" through virtual conference centers and virtual convention buildings to host virtual symposia, virtual exhibitions[36] and virtual summits. To navigate these realities in VR, Avatars will be mainstream, together with their market niche of fashion, clothing, accessories, and luxury, providing designer outfits both in virtual and in person. Mind that events will still be attended in person and business travel will still maintain its attractiveness; events will simply be experienced in all versions of reality – augmented, virtual, mixed and extended. Avatars and VR will be an irresistible force for *Dematerialized Work* to happen, sustained by the branded digital infrastructure and the reputation factor coming with the VR presence in business events. Connecting through Avatars in 2030 will be the equivalent of connecting through WhatsApp in 2020. With a permanent online presence, the two parts of identity and corporeality originally cleaved together for job interviews and contracts will be cut, and work will possibly be given to Avatars in a process never leaving cyberspace.

Second, technologies will sever nationality from territoriality. Modern countries rest on the concept of Westphalian "nation-states", places composed of ethnic group histories, limited by physical geographic borders, and based on centralized governance. Depending on your citizenship, you may be subjected to certain duties (such as taxes or laws) for which, in exchange, you may receive public services – including to some extent general welfare and protection. The so dear Westphalian sovereignty, with each state having exclusive sovereignty over its territory, will have to be re-thought in a world where space has not the same meaning and sometimes has no meaning, such as in cyberspace. In this concept of the world, laws and regulations can seep in from paths never thought possible until 2030. Since there is, in all respects, an overlay from cyberspace to the territorial governance, nationality is no longer bound to physical constraints. Digital nations could be on the rise. Look at Estonia, as an example. This Baltic state is the first nation in the world to provide "e-Residency", a digitally issued ID which empowers any global citizen to run a location-independent business, pay taxes, and to access a wide range of government-related services. Another innovative state, Bermuda, is experimenting along the same lines with the idea of Citizen Authentication. They will provide Identity-as-a-Service, in which they become an authenticator of identity data so that system participants inside or outside their country can access an array of services. Projects such as these are setting the first boundaries in a race towards virtual nations – a system of cloud-scale services provided by governments to stakeholders beyond their national or ethnic citizenship.[37] It is crucial to note here that a virtual nation will not necessarily overthrow the current nation-state system[38]; it could integrate it with different "layers of service". For instance, nothing would stop anybody to be a Swiss citizen and a virtual nation resident at the same time. Pension service could be provided by Switzerland, healthcare assistance by a virtual nation, and travel visa documentation by another. Or (as it is possible already) be a Brazilian citizen with an e-Residency that gives your business access to the European market. Individuals may choose which virtual nation(s) to be part of, depending on their specific needs and on available options. A virtual state population could be ultimately self-selecting communities already gathering digitally through platforms to manage themselves. Some even vote or maintain governance systems, just like physical states do. The new virtual nations will need a complex platform offering digital identity, currency, distributed governance systems, an economy, community services, even an identifiable culture. If it sounds familiar, that is because it is. With its 2.5 billion users, Facebook is the largest digital platform worldwide, offering a currency (Libra), a distributed governance service (bot and moderators enforcing Facebook rules of conduct and Facebook community standards), an economy (the Marketplace), community services, and a distinct culture – it can be a short step to rebrand from a digital corporation to a digital nation. When physical distance is overcome, and there are no borders to stop

33   Floridi, L. (2017). Digital's cleaving power and its consequences. *Philosophy & Technology*, 30, 123–129.
34   Toffler, A. (1980). *The third wave*. London: Collins.
35   For example, on YouTube.
36   E.g. https://www.leonardodrs.com/naval-forces-virtual-tech-expo/.
37   Stalnaker, S. (2019). Crafting virtual nations. *Maize.io*.
38   Despite the clear implications for non-state actors.
39   Baldwin, R. (2019). Digital technology and telemigration. The future of services trade. (p.126). *World Trade Report 2019*.
40   Vandergheynst, P. (2020). EPFL Applied Machine Learning Days Event, AMLD 2020.
41   Diamandis, P.H., Kotler, S. (2012). *Abundance – The future is better than you think*. New York, NY: Free Press.
42   Minerva – Schools at KGI. https://www.minerva.kgi.edu/.
43   The spatio-temporal representation of the skills and competencies, their interaction with other professional and life experiences, in-loops and out-loops of postgraduate, postdoctoral, professional or executive education. The natural extension of the concept of skill-prints from Stanford 2025, described "As a unique, living artifact of competencies" – moving from bidimensional "prints" to 3D "sculptures", thus able to capture the temporal dimension of interconnections. Retrieved from http://www.stanford2025.com/axis-flip.
44   Like what happened to Klout, that had to restructure its business completely due to GDPR.

outsiders from coming, the concept of migration will wear a completely different meaning, to become "Telemigration".[39]

The so dear Westphalian sovereignty, with each state having exclusive sovereignty over its territory, will have to be re-thought in a world where space has not the same meaning and sometimes has no meaning, such as in cyberspace.

Third, technologies will disentangle education, learning, and academic degree. We no longer live in a world of asymmetrical and top-down information controlled by a few, but rather in a democratized knowledge abundance. Google has flattened the information resource chain, with a one-sided supply model no longer in existence. Learning is on the way toward breaking the classical unities of drama – unity of action, unity of place, and unity of time.[40] It will not need to take place in a classroom, and it might not even require teachers. On-demand knowledge is available, it is free, and it is fast. Technology now changes at a pace so rapid that even some skills taught in college become redundant or outdated by the time of graduation. This will be a Sputnik moment for education systems still rooted in conceptions dating back to the Eighties or even the Sixties, when the main concern pertaining to education was offering widespread access, not tailored refinement. In this sense, living this shift will be another indicator of global wealth and abundance in the sense of Diamandis.[41] Learning could be achievable without education, as information and structure are available out in the open. Education could be obtained outside the aegis of academia, through the countless new ways of transfer of knowledge, such as e-learning and MOOCs (massive open online courses), immersive virtual and augmented reality training experience, mentoring and reverse mentoring, and work shadowing or community of practice to name only a few. To compete in the future economy, professionals will need to be equipped with an elaborate list of soft skills, such as nuanced communication and negotiation, abstract problem solving, interdisciplinary learning, and civic responsibility – an argument so strongly contended that Minerva, a new four-year college program,[42] teaches its students precisely such skills. It will be crucial for people to learn their multiplier skill, their meta-skills, the skills they possess that can be transferrable to new businesses that have not yet been conceived. Academic degrees, conversely, could be obtained without the traditional meaning of "learning" and "education". Universities will have to evolve towards a different meaning of the certification they are giving, meaning less "education" and more "passport for the world of work". The concept of a skills portfolio will only be reinforced by the dynamic of tech-enabled pulverization of complex profiles, platformization of the economy and taskization. Equally, these drivers will underpin the emerging concept of talent curation and "skill-ptures",[43] to bring skills development as easy and accessible as exploring new suggested songs on Spotify or new TV series "for you" on Netflix, to bring up profiled notifications like "You know X, Y, Z: others who know X, Y, Z also know W" or "Based on your skills fingerprint, why don't you learn X?". In such a manifold scenario, influence and peer recognition will be more important than ever, up to the point of becoming a metric, while keeping in mind the lessons of the past[44] to be privacy- and identity-preserving.

3. Community

The future will be happening at a very high speed. Transitions that we are now seeing just at the horizon are incoming unimaginably fast. The trait of futures *More, Faster* implies radical disruptions for companies and organizations that have to first cope, then manage, and eventually shape the impact these forces are impressing on them. Not every organization will be able to respond to this existential call to action in the same way. The largest will be able to undertake this endeavor alone, having at their disposal the necessary resources, competences and resolve; others will have to muster to share burdens and talents – like with the concept of Living Labs, where different organizations share space, ideas, resources, and risk to overcome a challenge that is beyond the reach of the resources of any single one.

Enabling this trait even more is the pulverization of job profiles, being ground down by connectivity everywhere and the capacity of interweaving single vertical skills brought about by *Digital's Cleaving Power*, and the resulting servitization and taskization. Companies will not need to find a single candidate whose profile is matching all the requirements for a position, rather they will be able to decompose the figure they are looking for into many single-task positions à la Lego bricks and then launch a talent hunt for those single specific pieces. In this manner, organizations and other entities will be able to tap into world-class talent in each individual single skill or task and then gather them together. The radical shift here is that we are observing another "cut and paste" executed by *Digital's Cleaving Power* – violating the unity of "job profile" into a "job" and several "profiles". In this way, companies might employ people for single tasks to be then

Companies will not need to find a single candidate whose profile is matching all the requirements for a position, rather they will be able to decompose the figure they are looking for into many single-task positions à la Lego bricks and then launch a talent hunt for those single specific pieces.

employed in several positions (e.g. a very keen ability with precision hand movements) and not for roles (e.g. surgeon, illustrator, welder, horologist). This will entail important consequences for Human Resources, as they will have to move from a one-dimensional concept of "job profile tied to an individual" towards multi-dimensional thinking needed to match a profile with the skills and tasks needed and the individuals possessing them. In this sense, the HR function will find itself right in the middle of this transformation, being the boundary converging the monolithic, transversal request for a profile from the organization and the single vertical possibilities coming from the skills/tasks market. The role of HR will not thus be centralized anymore but will remain central, working as a nexus to synchronize all the requests from the community, distribute loads and harmonize growth. The capacity to weave single vertical "forte" together will open up an immensely broader pool where to look. While large industries and organizations might have enough resources to tackle this transformation alone and be able to still attract the talent they need from a widely diverse audience than the one they were used to source, in SMEs talent will be shared across a community and sourced from a common pool, as smaller players in the world of work will not have the necessary leverage on good talents otherwise. Dematerialization of work will empower a flatter organization giving room to informal organizational units to manage their operations "at the edge" of the company, as in a hybrid ambidextrous structure,[45] much like their information and digital connection, that will happen at the edge of the network.[46] The flexibility, pervasiveness, availability, and security of the network will enable a different, unconventional and sometimes unorthodox working paradigm based on radical agility and dispersion across the geographic location.[47] Movement of individuals will not be necessary anymore as the organization will "be everywhere and anywhere" but with almost no physical locations. Even flagship headquarters, conference centers, auditoriums, and boardrooms will be virtual, designed by exclusive digital architects augmented by AI providing extreme uniqueness to each design,[48,49] and with potentially no respect for the laws of Nature that vex their creativity in the physical realm of the world. Communities of SMEs, or of informal units "at the edge" from larger companies, may find a natural self-organization in "professional families" and build a value network up to even larger crowds, arranging themselves into cross-national and even supra-national organizations. Through easier access to talent, jobs and tasks, workforce will grow stronger into its self-awareness of being a global community.

45   Tushman, M.L. & O'Reilly III, C.A. (1996). Ambidextrous organizations: Managing evolutionary and revolutionary change. *California Management Review*, 38(4). ABI/INFORM Global.

46   Reznik, A. (2018, 14 May). What is edge? ETSI Blog.

47   D'Alessandro, J. (2020, 26 June). Dallo smart working al south working. Per lavorare a Milano vivendo a Palermo. *La Repubblica*.

48   Schnabel, M.A. (2007). Parametric designing in architecture. In *Computer-Aided Architectural Design Futures (CAADFutures)* (pp. 237–250). Dordrecht: Springer.
     Dino, I. (2012). Creative design exploration by parametric generative systems in architecture. *METU Journal of Faculty of Architecture*, 29(1), 207–224.
     Jabi, W. (2013). *Parametric design for architecture*. Laurence King Publishing.

49   Algorithmic design is not simply the use of a computer to design architecture and objects. Algorithms allow designers to overcome the limitations of traditional CAD software and 3D modelers, reaching a level of complexity and control which is beyond the human manual ability, towards the concept of Digital Architecture. Algorithms-Aided Design employs design methods that allow users to research new formal and production solutions through the use of generative algorithms, exploring accurate freeform shapes through computational techniques to develop and control complex geometries, such as high-formal-complexity parametric modeling, digital fabrication techniques, form-finding strategies, environmental analysis and structural optimization.
     See Tedeschi, A. (2014). *AAD: Algorithms-aided design: Parametric strategies using Grasshopper*. Le Penseur.

4. Trust

When your workforce is geographically dispersed, radically agile and following unorthodox schemes in achieving objectives through agility and creativity, the good old 9 to 5 "badge-in, badge-out" has simply no sense anymore. There cannot be a "control" of the workforce as it was in the years of the second Industrial Revolution, when all knowledge and production assets had to be centralized because of capital intensity and energy consumption. Paradigms rooting in shallow quantitative metrics like elapsed time or money spent are basing their existence on an assumption of linearity, both of results and with regards to the context that is being crushed by the digital tsunami[50] we are living.

Taskization and servitization destroy the idea of key performance indicators (KPIs) from the Sixties, imposing an overcoming of the thousand-mile screwdriver syndrome,[51] also called "uber-micromanagement",[52] as both time and money are employed by workforce and management in a completely different way. These resources will no longer be used linearly, with a simple one-dimensional cause-effect relation – work will no longer be traded along the traditional "time for money" exchange. Time and money instead will lie in a complex multi-dimensional value web, as individuals will no longer have job families based on training and experience and be employed for them, but rather will have a portfolio of skills, competencies, require-ments, and needs creating invisible economies and informal networks in life, online, and onlife.

The value web of their work, then, will present several overlaps, namely ambiguities, in its description or requirement of resources, due to the different description, unbundling, allocation, execution and re-composition of an objective or a profile in single tasks and skills. Willing or not, organizations will have to gear themselves and the top management with ways to transform their posture towards a more empowering and empowered by Trust. With the value of time and the meaning of jobs being disrupted, complexity will increase and transparency will decrease. Trust will be the key ingredient for a smoothly functioning world of work.

This will not be the only radical change impressed on the trust landscape by the incoming tidal wave of digital. In 2030 new network and infrastructure access paradigms will be the root cause and shaping force of the advent of Data Oceans.[53] In parallel, a new current of security concerns and concrete massive security threats will rise, due to the omnipresent, global, and permeating presence of the digital and cyber dimension into everyone's life. Cybersecurity will clearly play a crucial role in supporting and driving the adoption of devices granting extremely fine-grained analytics on personal and professional life. These tools will improve working performance, something constantly sought after in a world even more globalized and with worldwide competition.

The act of building trust in the infrastructure will inevitably have to align the stars of "security by definition",[54] "ethics by design",[55] and "trust by operation" to safeguard users, machines and other sources of data against illegitimate of malicious use of their systems, data, information, and most importantly, identity. At the same time organizations willing to exploit the immense informational resources lying in Data Oceans will have to respond meaningfully to the significant calls for trust

in the collection, management and deletion of data. It will give rise to potentially complicated legal landscapes, with the novel institutional and regulatory framework that more advanced nations will likely design to cope with major shifts in jurisprudence. Organizations must confront these new vistas with consistent technological anticipation to be able to have solutions at hand and compliant "at day zero".

Willing or not, organizations will have to gear themselves and the top management with ways to transform their posture towards a more empowering and empowered by Trust.

Some examples of the challenges already surfacing are the right to be forgotten and data sovereignty, for which we must encompass a structured approach to factor in these elements in the equation of trust building. Security, ethics, and trust in network, infrastructure, and technology will bring along data protection almost as a corollary. With trust endowed in the foundations of the instruments, real-time collaboration will open up, bringing explosive opportunities for exponential knowledge creation in virtual, augmented and extended space. Technology will dispossess physical distance of meaning through the enablement of comprehensive, holistic, organic data and information sharing. Push it more, faster, and it goes up to a potential outright brain-computer integration, only being possible thanks to the effort in granting security, ethics, and trust in the infrastructure and the technologies underpinning it.

This revolutionary technological avalanche will enable a seamless and boundaryless remote real-time collaboration environment that could be at least as effective as in-person, if not more, thanks to virtual and extended reality technologies. These characteristics will even more empower open access to data, while laying the technological groundwork on which the body of law can ensure there is no misuse. It will not be far-fetched to envision a governing body for data, and not just personal data; scientific data will also be encompassed, as the fundamental enabler for exponential knowledge creation.

The theme of trust will also be crucial in the realm of transparency of information, with the creation of information "pedigrees" guaranteeing traceability back to the source and granting a record of the assumptions taken to draw conclusions. While this might seem strict and even exaggerated today, note that information comes from data; with the unimaginable volume, variety and value of data available in a Data Ocean, in there it might be possible to "fish" any information.

Algorithms here will play a fundamental part and will be a crucial asset for organizations, entities, even governments. Algorithms will have the potential to be what nuclear weapons were during the Cold War, chemical weapons were in the Eighties and Nineties, and cyber weapons were during the first two decades of the 21st century. In this sense, and due to their proneness to be easily weaponized, like most of cyberspace, there will be two different currents fueling forces in action in the future. On the one side, there will be an algorithm economy around the concept of exponential knowledge creation and

50   Albert, S. (2018, 30 August). Are we ready for the digital tsunami? *The Conversation.*

51   Witness to the interaction between the National Command Authority (NCA) and the on-scene commanders during the Saigon forces evacuation, Admiral Metcalf coined the phrase "six-thousand-mile screwdriver" – the minute direction of the day-to-day operations of a field commander by higher and remote authority. See Cummings, J.J. (2003). *Does network centric warfare equal micromanagerial warfare? Minimizing micromanagement at the operational level of war.* Naval War College. Metcalf, J. (1986). Decision making and the grenada rescue operation. In J. G. March & R. Wessinger-Baylon (Eds.), *Ambiguity and Command.*

52   Noguchi, Y. (2017, 17 July). Is your boss too controlling? Many employees clash with micromanagers. *NHPR.* O'Connell, B. (2020, 31 March). Don't micromanage during the coronavirus. *SHRM.*

53   See *More, Faster,* p. 42.

54   "Formal Methods" refers to mathematically rigorous techniques and tools for the specification, design and verification of software and hardware systems. The phrase "mathematically rigorous" means that the specifications used in formal methods are well-formed statements in a mathematical logic and that the formal verifications are rigorous deductions in that logic (i.e. each step follows from a rule of inference and hence can be checked by a mechanical process.) The value of formal methods is that they provide a means to symbolically examine the entire state space of a digital design (whether hardware or software) and establish a correctness or safety property that is true for all possible inputs. However, this is rarely done in practice today (except for the critical components of safety critical systems) because of the enormous complexity of real systems. See Butler, R. W. (2016). *What is formal methods?.* Langley Formal Methods, NASA.

55   Tonkinwise, C. (2004). *Ethics by design, or the ethos of things.* Design Philosophy Papers, 2(2) 129–144.

56   The IEEE Global Initiative on Ethics of Autonomous and Intelligent Systems, *Ibid.*

57   Barber, L. (2017, 16 September). *Fake news in the post-factual age.* Lecture to Oxford Alumni Festival. See also Flood, A. (2016, 15 November). 'Post-truth' named word of the year by Oxford Dictionaries. *The Guardian.*

58   A recent review of the matter is in "Post-truth politics", *Wikipedia, The Free Encyclopedia.*

Data Oceans; on the other hand, to preserve trust in this very thin and fragile context, there will be the foundational need for algorithm vetting and ethically aligned design.[56]

In a world so easily stormed by data and information, human beings will try to find emotional shortcuts for sensemaking in such an overwhelmingly complex and overloaded world. Influence, thus, will be a game changer for organizations to build trust and reach the emotional part of their audience for amplified and empowered engagement. At the same time, with the risk of people detaching from factual evidence due to its unmanageable volume, organizations and influencer within and outside them will play a very delicate role in avoiding post-factuality[57] or post-truth.[58]

5. Centaurs & Knights

Humans build many different ways to reconcile the best of artificial and biological intelligence. One of the most relevant factors when it comes to a smooth integration of these two worlds is age. Older adults face unique barriers to adoption, ranging from physical challenges to a lack of comfort and familiarity with technology.[59] And indeed, an important challenge facing older adults with respect to technology is the fact that many are simply not confident in their own ability to learn, adopt, and properly use new technologies and electronic devices.[60] In 2017, some 34% of older internet users say they have little to no confidence in their ability to use electronic devices to perform online tasks, while 48% of seniors say that this statement describes them very well: "When I get a new electronic device, I usually need someone else to set it up or show me how to use it". This does not improve significantly in middle-aged users, where 62% find they need help in adapting new devices or technologies.[61] However, once past this first obstacle, senior or middle-age users on the internet tend to view technology in a positive light and incorporate digital technology into their everyday lives.[62] This trend will become even more significant due to the compression of time between generations – we will explore this concept later in this section. Anyhow, former generations will not, in most of the cases, be able to keep up with the pace of technology,[63] as waves of radically new technologies will come more often and faster. AI natives (those belonging to Generation Z – born after 1997 – and the subsequent Generation Alpha) will bring a range of tools with them, stemming from the profound integration of technology not just with their lives[64] but within themselves and their mind structure.[65] They will be born immersed in these tools, or even with them. For this very reason, they will potentially be in a situation of absolute conceptual dependency from these tools, likely being unable to conceive working, studying, communicating, or even connecting and partnering, without this technological dimension that will have accompanied them from birth. The most straightforward consequence is that their description of the world will be in terms of these tools,[66] as their experiential and cognitive economy will be administered through this technological filter. We will see

While former generations think in terms of online and offline, AI natives are onlife, in a hybrid status with blurred borders between being online and offline.

the summit of representation for the Third Dator's Law of the Future: "we shape our tools and therefore our tools shape us". It also comes of support to paraphrase Wittgenstein[67]: for those belonging to these newer Generations, "the limits of my tools are the limits of my world". The schism in the perception of the world and its consequent sensemaking, happening via a completely different route on the one hand for the older and middle-age components of the workforce, and on the other hand for the two newer cohorts, will bring to a radical separation in the conception and use of language, bringing even more distance to a panorama already severed. Some of the bargains and trade-offs the technologies of Gen Z and Gen Alpha will drive, or even impose, will be very natural to accept for the newer Generations while much more awkward

for the older. Sometimes the concessions required by these technologies will speak to a level Generation X and Millennials (or Generation Y) would not even completely understand, due to their physiological lagging to the adoption of leading-edge technologies. Both a cause and an effect will be a very different concept of privacy and life: while former generations think in terms of online and offline, AI natives are onlife,[68] in a hybrid status with blurred borders between being online and offline. It is the result of the blurring of the distinction between reality and virtuality, the blurring of the distinctions between human, machine and nature, the reversal from information scarcity to information abundance, and the shift from the primacy of entities to the primacy of interactions. It is a paradigm completely different from what Gen X and Gen Y conceived but that they themselves were key in creating. Organizational functions looking at the human angle in their geometries, and Human Resources especially, will have to look into creating a form of Generation management to have these visions coexist the best way possible,[69] to exploit the creative tension between these distant opposites for the creation of value in the organization. Part of this Generation management could include intergenerational solidarity, in the keeping of reverse mentoring but on a more personal and intimate plane – where reverse mentoring is about learning, solidarity is about identity. Inter-generational workforce management will be a key funnel for reskilling and upskilling of the entire workforce, to preserve and empower it to be modern and fresh. The use of AI for performance augmentation will be undeniable to keep the pace of a market asking *More, Faster*. The exponential pace of technology will reverb in this trait of futures as well, through its effect of exponential "compression of time", meaning

59 Anderson, M. & Perrin, A. (2017). *Tech adoption climbs among older adults.* Pew Research Center.
60 Anderson, M. & Perrin, A. *Ibid.*
61 Anderson, M. & Perrin, A. *Ibid.*
62 Anderson, M. & Perrin, A. *Ibid.*
63 Morris, M. & Venkatesh, V. (2000). Age differences in technology adoption decisions: Implications for a changing work force. *Personnel Psychology.* 53, 375–403.
64 Vogels, E. A. (2019, 9 September). Millennials stand out for their technology use, but older generations also embrace digital life. *Pew Research Center.* FactTank.
65 Ruggieri, M. & Sammino, G. (2017). Body as a network node: Key is the oral cavity. In S. Dixit & R. Prasad (Eds.), *Human bond communication: The holy grail of holistic communication and immersive experience.* Wiley.
66 Vigo, J. (2019, 31 August). Generation Z and new technology's effect on culture. *Forbes.*
67 The original quote is "The limits of my language are the limits of my mind. All I know is what I have words for". Wittgenstein, L. (1921). *Tractatus Logico Philosophicus.*
68 Floridi, L. (Ed.). (2015). *The onlife manifesto.* Cham: Springer International Publishing.
69 Meyer, J. (2011). Workforce age and technology adoption in small and medium-sized service firms. *Small Business Economics,* 37, 305–324.
70 According to Oxford Languages, the Silent Generation is "the generation of people born before that of the baby boomers (roughly from the mid 1920s to the mid 1940s), perceived to tend towards conformism or restraint in their outlook and behavior".
71 Dimock, M. (2019, 17 January). Defining generations: Where Millennials end and Generation Z begins. *Pew Research Center.* FactTank.
72 This is a consequence coherent with the implications of the exponential pace of technology that entails an exponential compression of time.
73 Kasasa Research splits Generation Y into two (Gen Y.1 and Gen Y.2), of which Gen Y.1 spans just 4 years. See Kasasa Research. (2020, 22 July). *Boomers, Gen X, Gen Y, and Gen Z explained.*

the reduced timespan experienced between events representing relevant progress. Even "generation" will acquire a different meaning. By generation we mean the separation in time between two people such that something that the one can imagine and dare is completely unimaginable from the other (e.g. personal computers for the Silent Generation,[70] or smartphones for Baby Boomers). The conventional wisdom assigns 25 years to a generation; but the Silent Generation and Baby Boomers did not have this irreconcilable gap, so it is safe to state that our meaning of "generation" was two generations towards the middle of this past century, i.e. 50 years. Then it became just one generation – think of the "technological distance" between Baby Boomers and Generation X – so, 25 years. Then this span kept shortening[71] to 19, then 16, and we see today that two children that are just about 10 years apart are completely different in their approach to technology. This distance will shorten even more in the next 10 years[72] to reduce to 7 or even 4.[73] Waves of radical disruption will come less and less spaced, with the result of continuous shocks on the world of jobs, skills, and work. This will imply an increased number of "job identity" changes, implying deep and profound reskilling. Those either wealthy or willing to afford an AI "half-body" will evolve towards Centaurs; the AI natives of Gen Z and Gen Alpha will almost entirely fall into this category. Others (including Gen X and Gen Y) with extensive training and possibilities offered by *Digital's Cleaving Power* will take the reins as Knights.

New competences
are the cause
and the consequences
of future innovations.

Quentin Ladetto
armasuisse S+T, *Foresight & Research Director*

6. Dematerialized Work

The tides of disruption happening across the human, social, technological, and economic environment will not leave the ontological dimension of labor untouched. Work will not just change its epistemology, or broadly speaking its "character", to phrase it in a way of Clausewitzian memory.[74] It will go through a process of transformation of its very meaning. Forces pushing in this process will be the aforementioned three -zations[75]:

Hundreds of millions of service-sector and professional workers in advanced economies will – for the first time ever – be exposed to the challenges and opportunities of globalization.

pulverization, taskization, servitization. In a world where job profiles are passé, the market will sink traditional professional figures for unorthodox combination of skills woven together in a bundle, not a person. That will be new normal in 2030, surpassing the comfortable idea of finding a single individual able to satisfy all the requirements for the position. While searching for a one-to-one match between job and applicant was an everyday business in the 2020s, in the 2030 timeframe staffing "the one candidate" will be as hard as finding the needle in a haystack. The multiplication of different technologies available and the shaping force exerted from them onto the world of work will require from both candidates and recruiters to be proficient or conversant in many more different aspects, faster than ever before. The detachment of requirements and expectations from what the labor market will offer, at a given price, will become so unmanageable to the point of forcibly embracing the three -zations to source the adequate level of fresh professionalism from the market. As a consequence, management will have to embrace untraditional concepts and paradigms to understand and manage this profound change in how the very human capital is framed. For instance, imagine leading across cyberspace a team with an impressively diverse background and profiles that are brought together just for a very specific task of which each of them provides just a very specific and vertical competence, like fibers in thread. Or assessing performances of teams that are not just virtual or in-person, neither online nor in life, but onlife,[76] founding their existence on *Digital's Cleaving Power*.

Dematerialization of work will also expand the relevance of two opposing trends. On the one hand, being able to disregard the physicality of knowledge workers will empower their sourcing from everywhere in a nation or even worldwide. *More, Faster* connectivity available even more throughout the globe[77] will give employers access to an unprecedented network of workers within national virtual borders and to refined expertise not otherwise reachable, as maybe located in a remote part of the physical world. That would result in a potential increase in national autonomy, stemming from the force of *More, Faster* and *Digital's Cleaving Power*. On the other hand, the increased interconnectedness and reliance on cyberspace infrastructure and technologies to enable such access would also entail an increased global dependence, in terms of skills and "mutually assured technologies"[78] as well. These two apparently discordant directions will find reconciliation in the emerging phenomenon of people working in a different nation from where they are physically located,

called "telemigration". Telemigration[79] is the result of the convergence of the three -zations at scale. Imagine pulverization, taskization and servitization expanding up to global reach and widespread access. Pulverization, consisting of the technology-mediated capability to unbundle complex profiles into a set of simpler and very limitedly connected tasks, could tap into a much richer base of possibilities, coming from an array of cultures.[80] Taskization, that is the possibility to re-build complexity into high-level profiles starting from a pulverized set of tasks, could enjoy a broader solution space to select what resulting profiles are acceptable and what are not. And servitization, powered by globalization, would bring an omnipresent platform where making everything happen. This will result in the next, inhumanely accelerated phase of more, faster globalization, as *Digital's Cleaving Power* will allow arbitrage of international wage differences without the physical movement of workers. While the first three waves of globalization[81] were mainly a concern of people who "made things" for a living (since globalization focused on things that we made), Globalization 4.0[82] will have the service sector in its crosshair. Hundreds of millions of service-sector and professional workers in advanced economies will – for the first time ever – be exposed to the challenges and opportunities of globalization. Conversely, this paradigm will allow less developed countries in rapid growth to access a panorama of resources previously unreachable because of unattractiveness of other accessory conditions related to the work environment or the ecosystem. Instead, the very much sought-after intellectual élites will have the option to telemigrate to more flourishing and developing economic grounds, thus creating a movement of a reverse brain drain into "brain retain" and "brain gain".[83]

Among all those in the élites, a special position of advantage will be retained from those able to have a preferential access and unparalleled vistas on the space of data and information. Centaurs and Demigods, then, will most of the time start from a leading position, and will in general have an edge. Data Oceans will enable access to discipline usually inaccessible to information mining, like mathematics, physics, chemistry, and biology, thanks to *Digital's Cleaving Power*, new access paradigms and the integration of AI in every aspect of our cognitive economy.[84] Hard sciences in general, thus, will start to experience research freelancers and an increased crowdedness of the research scene, up to that moment very disciplined.

The HR function, as the human frontier between the individual and the organization, will have to harness at least a part of this disruption, incorporating elements of these paradigms into itself. One of the ways of doing this could be moving to a paradigm of a distributed HR, finding support in the resurgent *Community* paradigm arising in these evolving times. The idea of unbundling HR to crowdsource all the best opportunities in the shared[85] common workforce and talent base (or talent pool) will likely be pursued from companies unable to sustain the costs of a radical re-think of HR. Indeed, realistically, besides large industries and multinational corporations, what HR function could really feature elements of telemigration in its current structure? Human Capital management will become so complex, once globalized and dematerialized, that HR itself will undergo a servitization, along the lines of the already ongoing HR Business Process Outsourcing (HR BPO). Much like transport, logistic, and supply chain industries boomed surfing on the first waves of globalization in the physical world,

74   Carl von Clausewitz speaks about the nature of war, which is due to human nature and always stays the same; and the character of war, which is the "how you wage war", which changes over time. Drawing upon this famous example, we are arguing that it's not just the character of work that is changing (or its epistemology), it is also the nature (its ontology). See von Clausewitz, C. (1984). *On war*, M. Howard & P. Paret, (Trans. Eds.). Princeton: Princeton University Press.

75   See *More, Faster*, p. 42.

76   Floridi, L. (Ed.) (2015). *The onlife manifesto*. Cham: Springer International Publishing.

77   Mosher, D. (2019, 16 May). Starlink: How SpaceX's 12000-satellite internet network will work. *Business Insider*. Bates Ramirez, V. (2020, 12 July). Google loon is now beaming wifi down to earth from giant balloons. *Singularity Hub*.

78   Like the Internet. The naming comes from "mutually assured destruction", the deterrence concept of the Cold War, but with a technological lens (i.e. technologies that if disrupted would take us back to the stone age). The more we advance in human progress, the more exponentiality and convergence interact, and the longer this list will be.

79   Baldwin, R. (2019). *The globotics upheaval: Globalization, robotics, and the future of work*. Orion Publishing Group. See also Nelson, E. (2019). *Globots and telemigrants: The new language of the future of work*. Quartz.

80   Culture plays a role in influencing development of some skills over
      others. Think naively of something deeply cultural, like food: we have
      chopsticks in China, knife and fork in Europe (for instance). In Europe
      there are peculiarities, like rolling spaghetti in Italy, cutting cheese in
      France, dunking bread in boiling cheese with a fourchette à fondue in
      Switzerland. As well, in the Asian region, there are similar peculiarities:
      chopsticks in China are different from those in Japan (where they are
      shorter) and Korea (where they are much heavier, as they are made
      of stainless steel – and there is a spoon for rice in Korea). Resulting
      fine-grained motility is completely different. Look also at the art of
      calligraphy in Japan, that is radically different from calligraphy in Europe:
      completely different pattern for hands. See Gandon, E., Nonaka, T.,
      Sonabend, R. & Endler, J. (2020). Assessing the influence of culture on
      craft skills: A quantitative study with expert Nepalese potters. *PLOS ONE
      Education Research*. Note also that this is not limited to hand-eye coordi-
      nation or craft skills: Chinese, Japanese, Korean and Turkish use simpler
      number words and express math concepts more clearly than English,
      making it easier for small children to learn counting and arithmetic. See
      Fuson, K.C. & Li, Y. (2009). Cross-cultural issues in linguistic, visual-quan-
      titative, and written-numeric supports for mathematical thinking. *ZDM
      Mathematics Education*, 41, 793–808, and the subsequent interview
      in Shellenbarger, S. (2014). The best language for math. *The Wall Street
      Journal*.
81   Baldwin, R. (2018). *If this is Globalization 4.0, what were the other three?*
      World Economic Forum Global Agenda blog.
82   Baldwin, R. (2018). *Ibid.*
83   European Committee of the Regions, Fondazione FORMIT, Progress
      Consulting S.r.l., and Università degli Studi Internazionali di Roma. (2018).
      Addressing brain drain: The local and regional dimension. EU: Publications
      Office.
84   See AI & Humans, p. 70.
85   Keep in mind the force of servitization of the economy, or "Gig economy".
      The "Exclusive" workforce will be a chimera for some companies.
86   "HR as a Service" hosted in the cloud, as in SaaS, "Software as a Service".
87   HR BPO and HRaaS Solution. Improve business results through holistic talent
      management of people, processes, tools, and analytics with HR as a Service
      (HRaaS). Conduent.
88   Deceptive, Disruptive, Digitized, Demonetized, Dematerialized, Democra-
      tized. Only the last four are relevant to our analysis as supporting forces of
      exponential trends. See Diamandis, P. H. & Kotler, S. (2015). *Bold: How to go
      big, create wealth and impact the world* (Exponential Technology Series).
      Simon & Schuster.

new dematerialized services, including HR, will be created for
this last wave of globalization hitting the service sector.
HRaaS[86] as a cloud-based HR Management System, will offer
end-to-end HR BPO[87] on a global scale, including traditional
HR services, and also worldwide skills curation and brokering.

Dematerialization of work will carry a remarkable and disruptive
impact on organizational processes, skill profiles, and personal
connections. Pulverization and taskization, in fact, will render
impossible for a traditional HR to have a holistic framing of
an individual, as there would just be an evaluation of specific
task performance (or the pertinence and performance in the
specific bundle of tasks). Human Resources, and talent management more specifically, will risk missing out on the evaluation
of new potentials linked to an individual.

In Diamandis' approach to exponentiality – his so-called
Six Ds[88] – digitalization, democratization, dematerialization,
and demonetization play the lion's share in pinpointing trends
that have the potential for evolving towards exponential growth,
or are on an exponential track already. As work is getting more
digitalized, democratized, and dematerialized at every step
we make towards 2030, it will become more exponential.
We will assist then not only to an increase in quantity, quality,
and wealth produced, but also in the actual speed of work.
Dematerialization will allow datafication,[89] that will in turn
empower more, faster machine analytics and intelligence on
the job. Software in the Twenties powers machine speaking,
reading, writing, reading handwriting, generating PowerPoint
presentations, even booking an appointment for a haircut.[90]
In the Thirties it will grow to take over the so-called "gateway

skills" that are exactly why humans were involved in many service office jobs today. Somebody has to open up the email or answer the phone and figure out what people want. In 2030, machines will do that. These white-collar-level machines will be "software robots" in the sense that they will be as effective as a human replacement, but without any physical presence or corporeity, while being part of the workforce. The very concept of workforce will then have to evolve towards including not just humans, but also autonomous and intelligent systems, and all the nuances in-between, such as Centaurs. This novel "digital workforce"[91] will wreak havoc on an unprepared HR function caught off-guard. We can very well expect digital workforces and telemigration to rightly be prominent in the dematerialized labor market of the future. And, more importantly, because we could get to have the work without the workers.[92]

As work will be dematerialized, datafied, and disrupted in its meaning, it might be worth considering a rethink of the value of work, as its inputs and outputs will have no corporeity anymore. Will there be a potential renewed interest for non-dematerialized occupations? And the moment work is dematerialized, will workers be invisible? Will we be leaving someone behind? These deep questions will be faced not just by HR leaders and managers, but by senior leaders in governments and politics as well. Dematerialization will also show its bright side to communities, as dematerializing means increasing the ability of producing closer to the customer. Think of metal 3D printing as an example: having just a digital file – and a 3D printer in place – will mean substituting all the intermediate steps of the metallurgic transformation, that will instead happen in loco with high-power lasers just to focus

89   Cukier, K. & Mayer-Schoenberger, V. (2013). *Ibid.*
90   Leviathan, Y. & Matias, Y. (2018, 8 May). Google Duplex: An AI system for accomplishing real-world tasks over the phone. Google AI Blog. Garun, N. (2019, 9 May). One year later, restaurants are still confused by Google Duplex. The Verge. Impressive recordings shared here: Chen, B. X. & Metz, C. (2019, 22 May). Google's Duplex uses A.I. to mimic humans (sometimes). *The New York Times.*
91   See "digital workers", in Baldwin, R. (2019). *The Globotics upheaval. Globalization, robotics and the future of work* (p. 7). Oxford: Oxford University Press. See also a complete definition in *HelpSystems Blog.* (2017, 20 July). How to build and scale a digital workforce.
92   Nelson, E. (2019). *Ibid.*
93   Contrary to intuition, it is indeed possible to 3D-print an I-beam. And by the way, 3D-printed I-beams have extraordinary properties inherited by the possibility of being created additively, instead of subtractively. See for instance the research of the chair for Digital Building Technologies at the Institute of Technology in Architecture, ETHZ. Retrieved from https://dbt.arch.ethz.ch/project/3d-printed-reinforced-beam/.

Dematerialization, with more, faster access and connectivity, will also allow "mirror cities" to exist in different climates, where temperatures will likely remain amenable despite global warming.

on one technique among the many available. All the work could happen collaboratively in cyberspace on a digital twin of the product. With just the raw materials being necessary to the creation of the final product, and with no need to exchange semifinished products to be reworked and assembled, the only transfer of goods happening would be the one of raw materials (usually in the form of dust) that have wonderful totipotence. It does not matter whether you are printing an I-beam,[93] a wrench, a bolt, or a needle – the raw metal dust is the same. This would drastically reduce logistic complexity (making any shipping simply additive) and environmental impact as a consequence. The force of dematerialization and the enabler of widespread ultra-connectivity will thus allow bringing life and livelihood to secluded areas (think of inner mountainous Switzerland), allowing individuals to reconnect with nature and empowering a better distribution of density of population. Even academic research groups and schools, for instance, would have, overnight, the immense new availability of working spaces to take better advantage of each region's geography from a broader point of view. Dematerialization, with more, faster access and connectivity, will also allow "mirror cities" to exist in different climates, where temperatures will likely remain amenable despite global warming. With better work and health conditions, the result will be increased or sustained competitiveness.

7. AI & Humans

There is today a persistent narrative around AI being an existential threat to humankind,[94] to which many industry captains, scientists, and thinkers have subscribed.[95] However, as we made clear since the introduction, this is a narrative we find deeply misplaced. Instead, humans are underrated. Human touch is needed for babies to survive, and equally so for AI.[96] AI scales humans and it does it in several different ways.

AI scales humans up, making them able to retrieve information from oceans of publications and sources, employing the raw power of analysis and management of huge volumes of data flowing in at significant velocities and with broad variety.

AI scales humans out, since thanks to machine cognition and the free fall of small volume production costs driven by more and faster digitalization and its cleaving power, we are on track to make it possible to have almost countless different strategies for the same product, making it uniquely tailored to every single one's desires or needs. You can personalize something that was mass-produced before, and that accounts to style as well as medicine.

AI scales humans across, making interactions possible where they were not. For instance, for those unable to speak to each other in their different languages, there is real-time translation today that already has quite a number of success stories.[97] In the future, AI might be able to blend new senses with the ones we have, bridging new technology towards us in a way we can integrate it. This might make it possible, for example, to extend the range of touch (being able to perceive sub-micron differences in width or flatness), hearing (integrating ultrasound and infrasound in our normal range of hearing), or sight (overlaying infrared and ultraviolet on our view but avoiding a mental breakdown). It could also bring new senses, like absolute direction, or, more broadly, the detailed perception of the electromagnetic field.[98]

In the future, AI might be able to blend new senses with the ones we have, bridging new technology towards us in a way we can integrate it.

Lastly, *AI scales humans within*: with the potential to move our comprehension of ourselves to a completely different level. The modern paradigm of quantified self[99] is just an example. The datafication[100] of our perceptions and feelings, underpinning a potential revolution on how we behave. Imagine being able to quantitatively measure the excitement in a relationship, or the affinity with someone, or knowing how to measure the right moment to train, think, create, relax. Fitness bands and smartwatches are only the beginning. More, and more complex sensors will come faster than we imagine, packed in even smaller forms with batteries lasting days or months, or without batteries altogether and powered by our bodies (motion, heat, chemical reaction, nerve endings…). Another example from today on how AI can scale humans within is through the identification, treatment and recovery from Post-Traumatic Stress Disorder (PTSD).[101] It was shown that participants who thought they were talking with the virtual

therapist alone were significantly more likely to open up.[102] For civilians, at least, just removing the idea of human presence led to more fruitful clinical sessions.[103]

AI and humans have several ways to interact with one another in different scenarios. The easiest we can think of is about alternance or "passing the baton" from AI to humans, back and forth. In this first one, humans do something and then AI does something, like with autonomous driving, that passes the control back to the human whenever it is stuck or is faced with a situation it can't solve. Not every step, however, can be taken as two separate entities: AI and humans can also work in symbiosis – a route we are tracing since the chapter on Mythology. An outstanding example of how this symbiosis happens is in the field of architecture: buildings don't have straight lines anymore. Look, for instance, at Zaha Hadid's The Opus in Dubai. AI provides new methods for validation of structural stability, thus enhancing breakthroughs in architecture. Or take the concert hall Elbphilharmonie by Herzog and De Meuron in Hamburg. It is covered with 10,000 tiles, each different from one another. The auditorium (the largest of three concert halls in the Elbphilharmonie) is a product of parametric design,[104] a process by which designers use algorithms to develop an object's form. Algorithms have helped design bridges,[105] motorcycle parts,[106] typefaces,[107] even chairs.[108] In the case of the Elbphilharmonie, Herzog and De Meuron used algorithms to generate a unique shape for each of the thousands of gypsum-fiber acoustic panels that line the auditorium's walls like the interlocking pieces of a giant puzzle. To design the 10,000 unique acoustic panels, the architects worked with famed acoustician Yasuhisa Toyota, who created an optimal

94 Matz, C. (2018, 9 June). Mark Zuckerberg, Elon Musk and the feud over killer robots. *The New York Times*.

95 Kshirsagar, R. (2018, 1 July). Why many important minds have subscribed to the existential risk of AI. *Towards Data Science*.

96 *Gartner identifies the human touch as the strongest element in AI*. (2018, 6 November). Gartner press release.

97 Levy, N. (2019, 8 January). Google Assistant's new 'Interpreter Mode' serves as real-time translator for hotel guests. *GeekWire*.

98 Thaddeus-Johns, J. (2017, 6 January). Meet the first humans to sense where north is. *The Guardian*.

99 Ferriss, T. (2013, 3 April). The first-ever quantified self notes. *Tim Ferris Blog*.

100 Cukier, K. N. & Mayer-Schoenberger, V. (2013). The rise of big data: How it's changing the way we think about the world. *Foreign Affairs*, 92(3), 28–40.

101 Gonzalez, R. (2017). Virtual therapists help veterans open up about PTSD. *WIRED*.
     NYU Langone Health / NYU School of Medicine. (2019, 22 April). Artificial intelligence can diagnose PTSD by analyzing voices: Study tests potential telemedicine approach. *ScienceDaily*.

102 Gale M. L., Gratch, J., King & A., Morency, L.-P. (2014). It's only a computer: Virtual humans increase willingness to disclose. *Computers in Human Behavior*, 37, 94–100.

103 *Ibid*.

104 See also Tedeschi, A. (2014). *AAD: Algorithms-aided design. Parametric strategies using Grasshopper*. Le Penseur.

105 Stinson, L. (2013, 4 October). This Cloud-like bridge was created with an algorithm. *WIRED*.

106 Rhodes, M. (2015, 23 September). The bizarre, bony-looking future of algorithmic design. *WIRED*.

107 Stinson, L. (2015, 3 March). Harnessing algorithms to create shape-shifting typography. *WIRED*.

108 Rhodes, M. (2016, 3 October). So. Algorithms are designing chairs now. *WIRED*.

109 GeorgiaTech News Center. (2020). *Shimon: Now a singing, songwriting robot*. GeorgiaTech press release.

110 Sabina Aouf, R. (2017, 5 July). Controllable Third Thumb lets wearers extend their natural abilities. *Dezeen*.

111 See https://www.daniclodedesign.com/thethirdthumb.

112 Lloyd, J. (2020). 'Third thumb' human augmentation rewires the brain. *Science Focus*.

sound map for the auditorium, developing an algorithm that produced the panels, each with a unique shape and pattern, mapped to clear aesthetic and acoustic specifications. That is the exploratory power of the machine: being unencumbered by preconceptions, a generative algorithm can run wild, sifting through thousands of possible solutions, the performance of which it can assess digitally after the fact. One of the most surprising aspects of generative design is that it models objects that look incredibly organic, almost as though they were generated from the earth, rather than a string of a code. Taking a different look at things, it is actually unsurprising. Just like nature has optimized for weight and improved stiffness, so too have these algorithms. Like nature, generative design is about trying things out and seeing what works. Crucially, however, it does so over the course of a few hours, as opposed to a few million years. It can be seen essentially as running accelerated artificial evolution.

Exploiting the power of unrestricted inquiry in the algorithmic space from the machine, joined with the discretionary and critical intuition of the human, is what bring us to the next possible template of interaction, taking to the next level. We talked about scaling within. AI offers tailored methods for learning more, learning faster and forgetting less. There are plenty of learning apps already today; in 10 years' time the offer will not just be broader, with more apps, it will be directly plugged into our brain. But it's not just about learning more, it's about learning what we simply could not learn. For instance, Shimon, a robot from GeorgiaTech, plays jazz.[109] But with four hands! As a robot, it's not limited by human structure. At the moment, every "hand" has just two "fingers", but the principle is clear. Playing along with it gets to the next level of your experience. Another example is the Third Thumb,[110,111] a 3D printed thumb extension for the hand controlled by the feet. The project investigates the relationship between the body and prosthetic technology in new ways. It is part tool, part experience, and part research; a model to better understand human response to artificial extensions. The Third Thumb instigates a necessary conversation about the definition of "ability". The origin of the word "prosthesis" meant "to add, put onto"; so not to fix or replace, but to extend. The project is inspired by this word origin, exploring human augmentation and aiming to reframe prosthetics as extensions of the body. What is very intriguing here is that users of the Third Thumb experience a shift in the way their brain elaborates inputs and finds solution strategies.[112] Imagine if the Thumb could operate learning from our past choices and anticipate our next (i.e. could be an autonomous/intelligent Thumb). Another clear example comes from AlphaGo,[113] the software able to challenge human skill in the extremely complex game of Go. After a few matches against this unconventional adversary, Fan Hui, the European champion of Go at the time, opened his eyes. Fan Hui will tell you that after five months of playing match after match with AlphaGo, he sees the game completely differently. His world ranking has skyrocketed. And apparently, Lee Sedol (one of the world's best Go players) felt the same way after being defeated over five games against AlphaGo. In Game Two, the machine made a move that no human ever would.[114] And it was beautiful. As the world looked on, the move so perfectly demonstrated the enormously powerful and rather mysterious talents of modern artificial intelligence.

But in Game Four, the human made a move that no machine would ever expect. And it was beautiful too. So beautiful that Go players around the world dubbed it "God's Touch". Indeed, it was just as beautiful as the move from the machine,[115] no less and no more. It showed that although machines are now capable of moments of genius, humans have hardly lost the ability to generate their own transcendent moments. And it seems that in the years to come, as we humans work with these machines, our genius will only grow in tandem with our creations. Conversely, we have to ask: If Lee Sedol hadn't played those first three games against AlphaGo, would he have found God's Touch? The machine that defeated him had also helped him find the way. They can help us find "better us" and thereby get to the next level.

Following the summit, the creators of AlphaGo revealed AlphaGo Zero. While AlphaGo learned the game by playing thousands of matches with amateur and professional players, AlphaGo Zero learned by playing against itself, starting from completely random play.[116] This powerful technique is no longer constrained by the limits of human knowledge. Instead, the computer program accumulated thousands of years of human knowledge during a period of just a few days and learned to play Go from the strongest player in the world, AlphaGo. AlphaGo Zero quickly surpassed the performance of all previous versions and also discovered new knowledge, developing unconventional strategies and creative new moves, including those which beat the World Go Champions Lee Sedol and Ke Jie.[117] These creative moments give us confidence that AI can be used as a positive multiplier for human ingenuity.

AI thus has an impact on humans. There are some bright sides and some dark sides, but it is undeniable that humans perceive themselves differently when in tandem with an autonomous, intelligent machine. How would this transfer in the working environment ten years from now because of the existence and integration of AI in the workplace and in our lives?

More connectivity, more computing power and more data will open up the possibilities to have always-on virtual assistants that might also be programmed to a certain specific voice strategy. Permanent assistants would most certainly help in distributing and lowering the cognitive overload due to tight and fast context switches, but at the same time will induce a sort of transfer of responsibility to the machine. Those more leaning towards the integration side, like Demigods and Centaurs, will lead this process and will consciously manage the proportion of machine presence into their thought process. Those less prone to the presence of AI in their self and thought paradigm might instead drift unwittingly towards being more and more induced to deciding what the AI suggests and, eventually, being led by it in a sort of Minotaur syndrome. In this sense, AI would even surpass the promises illustrated in the previous paragraphs, but only for those able to channel them. This implies that AI assistant will need to exercise great care in user experience (UX) and profiling. Quantified self, while potentially bringing a revolution in the way we experience our inner and outer selves, might also take away the instinct of self-awareness, as there would be an "induced" awareness – further aggravated by its datafication, making it ready for consumption without any need for deep insight in our inner

113 See https://deepmind.com/research/case-studies/alphago-the-story-so-far.
114 Metz, C. (2016, 16 March). In two moves, AlphaGo and Lee Sedol redefined the future. *WIRED*.
115 Metz, C. (2016). *Ibid*.
116 Silver, D., Schrittwieser, J. & Simonyan, K. et al. (2017). Mastering the game of Go without human knowledge, *Nature*, 550, 354–359.
117 Chan, D. (2017, 20 October). The AI that has nothing to learn from humans. *The Atlantic*.

world. As a consequence, this might very well bring an impressive improvement in profound and broad insight for our inner self, but just for those actively looking for it and with the agency to interact positively with the AI counterpart. However, without these premises, this interaction might turn negative and result in a deficit in self-perception. The amplification of soft skills, something fully in scope with AI scaling humans up, might follow trajectories sometimes deadened by the ever-present use of machine cognition and Data Oceans. There would be a positive, anyway, as skills would be much more easily learned, unlearned, re-learned and right-learned. Importance and access to soft skills would grow, as a better expression of the purely human part. A soft skill upgrade would nevertheless be feasible and sought after (as AI scales humans up). Access to education, learning and development would be broad and ubiquitous; the same would be true for data, used to suggest and improve those courses taken by humans. As the knowledge base would be globalized, and the same could be said for the decision base on which the platform could suggest skills and development, there could be a risk of uniforming of thought, as in the reverberation chamber effect. On the other hand, such a widespread, collaborated, and curated source of learning for skills could be game-changing for the growth of countries traditionally "left behind" as well as for weaker social segments.

AI offers tailored methods for learning more, learning faster and forgetting less.

8. Opportunities

As explored in the Traits of Futures until here, the forces of Exponentiality and Convergence in their guise of *More, Faster* and *Digital's Cleaving Power* will have ample and vast consequences in the way we will perceive, make sense, frame and act upon what is around us, in every dimension of space – physical, cyber, information, cognitive. These consequences, despite being disruptive and transformational for any adult living in the Twenties (2020), will bring along plenty of positive ripples even in distant realms of our life in the Thirties (2030). The interconnection, dematerialization, datafication, virtualization, and the metamorphosis they will carry with them by the means of exponential technologies, will bring broad democratization and wider participatory democracy to the new, fresh, and different opportunities incoming.[118] Indeed, we will be seeing a steep increase in their volume, as the abundance brought by progress of humankind in 2030 and beyond unfolds[119] towards a world of post-scarcity.[120] *Opportunities* will take shape across time and space, and both from "more" and "less". We see four different pillars here, in the four paragraphs as follows.

More time. There will be more sand in the hourglass. A novel socio-technical continuum will offer possibilities for life-long learning and skilling in all their paradigms (declined as four prefixes[121]: new, re-, un-, right-). Education, new skills, and upskilling will be available, meaningful, and achievable throughout our entire life[122] and working curriculum,[123] that from the Twenties to the Thirties will enjoy a very significant extension. Moreover, the break of classical unities of study[124] and the subsequent makeover for nonlinearity in education, learning, and skilling, will offer the chance for extended time spans to achieve certifications when desired.

The leading way of augmenting and strengthening one's education and skills portfolio will be through bite-sized, granular achievements to be arranged in the frame of the development portfolio.[125]

More space. The value network will cross the boundaries of physical space to mesh with cyber, and a substantial part of it will reside in the virtual infrastructure. As the online and onlife paradigms give unprecedented freedom of access and room for maneuvering, even the most élite education institutions will need to pivot from their current in-person only models to at least differentiated offers for the same curricula. It would be a vital evolution, shifting significantly from just the current "X" versions of the offers available on online learning platforms such as edX or Coursera, towards a complete equivalence of the offer and of the certification achieved, if any, or the portfolio gained. Why would Ivy League-level schools like Harvard or Stanford maintain prestigious physical campuses when most of their paying students are online? The relocation of campuses and curricula to VR will give exclusive institutions boundary-less access to the best minds worldwide and create new opportunities to interact in VR. We could see the unfolding of a complex, evolving digital twin of the physical world – the Mirrorworld.[126] If there is another "our" world beyond, overlaid to our world, then who are we and where are we in this superposition of worlds? We can be more than ourselves, multiply our identities, or integrate all of them empowering reciprocally. More space will also be available for career progression, rendering them truly boundary-less, thanks to the cleaving operated by the digital dimension with respect to presence and locality. Novel technologies and their new

uses will enlarge the possibility space of its creative potential, as one of the several ways technology can scale people is up,[127] by leveling differences, softening hard inequalities and making up for disabilities. Technology opens up previously inaccessible domains to specific categories.[128] Looking at it through a Mirrorworld lens, it would also be conceivable to create places that exist neither in the real world nor in the physical world; we can do it nowadays already. Art, for instance, is a forerunner in this exploration of meaning in Augmented Reality.[129]

With more data, more access, faster responses and more compressed schedules, there will be an increased reliance on machine support to sift through this varied volume of possibilities.

Less time. The clock will need to tick less to get to the same destination. With more data, more access, faster responses and more compressed schedules, there will be an increased reliance on machine support to sift through this varied volume of possibilities, to pinpoint the optimal trajectories of development for talent, career, and education. The concept of a talent curator will become established by 2030, and not just for us, but also for our machine half (for AI natives of the likes of Demigods and Centaurs) or machine counterpart (for Knights). Machine intelligence and support, like AI, could provide sophisticated thinking skills and certain types of pattern recognition to average-skilled people, leading to semi-professional jobs

118 For instance, looking at how the Second Machine Age is unfolding in the broader framework of Machine Ages and Human Ages. For this framework, see Rizzo, G. (2019). Disruptive technologies in military affairs. In F. Rugge (Ed.), *The global race for technological superiority*. Washington, DC: Brookings Institution and ISPI. On the Second Machine Age, see Brynjolfsson, E. & McAfee, A. (2016). *The second machine age: Work, progress, and prosperity in a time of brilliant technologies*. W. W. Norton & Company.

119 Diamandis, P. H. & Kotler, S. (2012). *Abundance: The future is better than you think*. New York, NY: Free Press.

120 Bookchin, M. (1971). *Post-scarcity anarchism*. Berkeley, CA: Ramparts Press. See also Sadler, P. (2010). *Sustainable growth in a post-scarcity world: Consumption, demand, and the poverty penalty*. Surrey, England: Gower Applied Business Research. See also Drexler, E. K. (2013). Radical abundance: How a revolution in nanotechnology will change civilization. PublicAffairs.

121 See *AI & Humans*, p. 70.

122 Gratton, L. & Scott, A. (2016). *The 100-year life living and working in an age of longevity*. London: Bloomsbury.

123 Dede, C. J. & Richards, J. (Eds.) (2020). *The 60-year curriculum: New models for lifelong learning in the digital economy*. UK: Routledge.

124 See *Digital's Cleaving Power*, p. 46.

125 For instance, the Stanford 2025 project proposes the "open-loop-university" where students instead of receiving 4 years of education front loaded at the beginning of adulthood would then receive a lifetime of learning opportunities (in-loops) interleaved with working experiences (out-loops). The total in-loops would account for 6 years spread over a lifetime. See the website of the Stanford 2025 project: http://www.stanford2025.com/open-loop-university.

between doctors and nurses, between lawyers and paralegals, between architects and draftsman.[130] This will augment people to a great extent without the need of very scholarly and academic competence, and instead leverage strongly on their pragmatic, professional, and life experience. This would, on the one hand, raise the base level of competence, and on the other hand, compress the times for achieving an AI-native university degree. Looking at the evolution of artificial companions as parallel opportunity for their owners or partners, it is an idea that finds existence already in the language of 2020 (think of Alexa's "skills"), and even its roots in the late 1990s (looking at how the phenomenon of Tamagotchi changed a generation). The co-existence of the two development paths of human and machine will not just entail their evolution side-by-side: it will find a tremendous added value when their development paths will converge. Taking advantage of the machine and its human partner learning alongside and together, and planning synergies between machine evolution and its human's Aspirations & Life Design, would be a new and powerful way to manage and leverage change. This new nature of collaboration between human and machine will thus bring new ways to upskill.

Less space. Cyberspace is a space without space, where physical distance has little meaning. And we as humankind will rely more and more on this space we ourselves created. Less space is not just about ample and worldwide access to positions traditionally inaccessible due to the collapsing of meaning for physical distance, it also speaks to the creation of added value and opportunities that would be unthinkable without the interconnectedness created. To grasp its boundless potential and the game-changing consequences, think of the global response for a COVID-19 vaccine. Teams distributed across the whole world could work side-by-side almost as they were in the same laboratory. Global, effortless and immediate access would be a double-edged opportunity. For top talents, this would give the possibility for broader choice and more advanced, prestigious, and superior education, lower and mid-quartile profiles would just have more and cheaper competitors from developing countries coming from the fourth wave of globalization.[131]

126 Kelly, K. (2019). AR will spark the next big tech platform–call it mirror-world. *WIRED*. See also Bradshaw, T. (2020). Enter the mirrorworld: How virtual reality will shape the 2020s. *Financial Times*. The original work is from Yale computer scientist David Gelernter in Gelernter, D. (1993). *Mirror worlds*. UK: Oxford University Press.

127 See *AI & Humans*, p. 70.

128 For instance, look at carpentry, joinery and cabinetmaking. These are traditionally jobs requiring sheer strength over anything else to even start considering them. However, the joinery and cabinetmaking sectors have become highly robotized in recent years. This development has made it possible to increase the number of women in these trades, which was unthinkable a few years ago. The SwissSkills 2020 French-speaking Switzerland champion in the cabinetmaking section is for the first time a woman: Léa Coutaz, a young lady from Saint-Maurice. Robotization has therefore enabled women to gain access to these very physical jobs. This increase in gender diversity in the construction industry is of great benefit to companies. See more in Benninger, M. (2020). L'hybridation entre formation et innovation est au cœur du processus. *HR Today*.

129 Adobe has developed Aero, "the most intuitive way to build, view, and share immersive AR experiences", and has an "Adobe AR Residency" program, to support artists as they explored the cutting edge of what's possible in augmented reality. Over three years from 2018 to 2020, the program brought together 23 artists' creative processes within the product development process to explore the potential of this new medium and inform the development of Adobe Aero. See https://adobe.com/aero. See also Lee, D. (2019, 4 November). Adobe Aero turns Photoshop layers into interactive AR experiences. *The Verge*; and Lardinois, F. (2019, 4 November). Adobe launches Aero, its AR authoring app. *TechCrunch*.

130 Nelson, E. (2019). Globots and telemigrants: The new language of the future of work. *Quartz*.

131 Baldwin, R., (2018). If this is Globalization 4.0, what were the other three?, *World Economic Forum Global Agenda blog*. See also *Dematerialized Work*, p. 64.

9. Enabling Laws

Looking at all groups, organizations, entities, and concepts impacted by the tidal forces of technological acceleration and disruption, law and jurisprudence are among those less prepared to sustain a full-frontal impact with the inconceivably fast changes in the character of our way of life and the subsequent implications for the body of law and its interpretation. Partly due to a "natural time" for the body of law to adapt to the environment, and partly to the need of a clear understanding of the possibilities and the implications before drafting a legislation. This is something that reflects in lawyers' approach to risk, as "lawyers tend to want an idea to be fully developed before they'll invest in it, which precludes the iterative development that leads to startup success".[132]

The epistemology of jurisprudence carries the existential hiatus between the disruption's speed of light and the response's speed of law. As a predominant part of the business community calls for a simplification of the body of law, seen as impenetrable to common sense and not fit for the cyber-physical world we live in,[133] it will bridle the might of technology and globalization to shape a change in this direction. Globalization and technology have revolutionized markets, affecting everything from airline travel to cabs. Much like other traditionally unthinkable fields ripe for disruption, as cancer research, law will not be immune. Together with the necessity of Enabling Laws, there will be the need to enable the Law. Indeed, when it was their moment, cancer doctors from the world's top research institutions were among the first to recognize the broad implications of AI storming the field. They began working with the forerunners to sort through massive amounts of data to try to find new ways to diagnose and cure the disease. Once again, it is not AI versus humans, it is *AI & Humans*. Lawyers may be far more susceptible than physicians.[134] As a rules-based system, law is similar to chess in which Deep Blue prevailed against a human in 1997.

Law has ethics at its core,[135] so its existential impasse is clear given the current challenges to ethics.[136] How can we guide a systemic transformation to the normative complex when the ethic compass is itself unclear? That is part of the "Enabling the Law" that needs to be tackled by a broad community of diverse stakeholders. In times of exponential development and irresistible convergence, solutions to complex problems cannot be found by just one single way of thinking. Diversity is key.

The epistemology of jurisprudence carries the existential hiatus between the disruption's speed of light and the response's speed of law.

Where will lawmakers and policymakers have to start from, and to what extent and breadth, to make the two irreconcilable speeds meet, the slowness of evolution of law versus the velocity of an accelerating world? What perimeter will *Enabling Laws* need to encompass to dent the apparently ironclad oxymoron of laws in an algorithmic world? One of the tenets will be around guaranteeing more protection in the two immensely vast realms of data and social security, and more agency for mid- and lower-quartile profiles being hit by the fourth wave of globalization. A number of studies have shown[137] that workers laid off from manufacturing jobs who subsequently become reemployed earn in the medium term 20% less or even up to 35% less than they earned before they were laid off. It is becoming increasingly clear that business and government leaders underestimated the gaps between who would win and who would lose as a result of globalization. Any effort to build a new social contract will need to address these gaps. A way to be inspired is by the ambition and foresight shown by the UK Education Act in 1918, rendering education compulsory up to the age of 14, and then part-time compulsory up to 18. This reform arrived in the middle of the second industrial revolution, allowing young students to build more transversal skills and thus be ready for emerging new jobs. Some historians frame the Education Act as passed to help the new rules brought upon by Neoliberalism and the demands and requirements of imperialist national efficiency, with the improved welfare and education of working-class children and adolescents regarded in this way not only as a social obligation but also as a national asset to help offset the challenge of other national powers.[138] In this sense, with the Fourth Industrial Revolution in its full upkeep, governments could think of a Continuing Education Act, much like what is done in Singapore with SkillsFuture.[139]

The similarity with the past century keeps being compelling. Two years after the Education Act, the UK passed the Unemployment Insurance Act (1920), when the originally limited unemployment insurance program was extended to cover most industrial wage earners, right in the middle of the full-steam Second Industrial Revolution. What employment was more than a hundred years ago, in the 2030s woven with pulverization, taskization, and servitization, where there will be work but not employment, will be skills and competences for the Gig economy. Facing the Fourth Industrial Revolution, then, governments may consider to promulge a skills act for the assurance of always-relevant competences. Broadening the scope of the last century, at the same time in 1919, the International Labour Organization (ILO) was created. As part of the Treaty of Versailles that ended World War I, the signatories reflected the belief that universal and lasting peace can be accomplished only if it is based on social justice. Fast forward to the 2030s, and it may be time for a fresh look at the social contract for a version that is good for the era of "4.0".

The need for a new social contract is steadfast, bridging the need to encourage entrepreneurship to thrive in a growing Gig economy and the need to cover for the risks that a fully individualistic society carries.

A new skills insurance could be one of the facilities in this social contract update planning for a common pool to reskill and upskill society or take care of those beyond reskilling. And if degrees are no longer a proxy for competencies and potential,[140] a new legal framework for higher education will have to be developed. It is true as well that to be proactive in re-skilling, up-skilling, and right-skilling an entire society, naïve goodwill is not enough. That is where technology comes to help. Everywhere computing and access, combined with a trillion intelligent devices spread across the geography,[141] will render it potentially feasible to run a national "workforce analytics"

132 McArdle, E. (2015). The laws of adaptation. *Harvard Law Bulletin*, Fall 2015.
133 European Union's General Data Protection Regulation (GDPR) is an extremely remarkable exception to this statement. In perfect line with the times, it understands the cornerstone position data enjoys in the cyber economy and puts the power in the hands of the producers of these data, rendering them owners, and declaring that it does not matter where data is processed, it matters who or what produces them. Therefore, data produced by a European citizen are under European legislation, wherever processing might happen. Disentangling position and location, and recognizing that presence in cyberspace is not a location in the physical space, is one of the fundamental cleavings operated by the *Digital's Cleaving Power* that is perfectly captured by GDPR.
134 McArdle, E. (2015). *Ibid.*
135 Law is the codification of the implementation of ethics. Ethics is the first principle based on the foundational statement: "human life is precious". Morals is the implementation of ethics, the do's and don'ts that must be followed in order to not break the ethical principle: "you may not kill a person needlessly". One step further, we have the Constitution, the codification of ethics into legal or otherwise foundational documents. For instance: "All human beings are born free and equal in dignity and rights." Lastly, Law is the implementation of the constitution into something by which actions can be judged as guilty or not guilty. Example: "One that bereaves another person of their life shall be sentenced for murder to prison, for no less than 10 years and no more than 18 years, or for the remainder of their life".
136 Page, C. (2020, 1 October). AI has resulted in "ethical issues" for 90% of businesses. *Forbes*. Lewis, P. (2020, 14 October). Why good ethics are now big business–and how to embrace them. *Forbes*.

for a global labor "force", for targeted (re-)orientation and to keeping the relevance of people in a world where there will increasingly be work without workers.[142] However, this prodigious infrastructure will pose challenges not less important.

Firstly, from the *Enabling Laws* standpoint, everyone would be part of a transformational "skills journey". The choices suggested for education, jobs or careers would lead to opportunities maximizing one's potential and developing a mastery of skills. To meet challenges and achieve success, there would be the need for everyone to opt in. Everyone should chart their evolving skill-print[143] and their own paths through lifelong learning and skills mastery. The ultimate achievement would be to make every job, every education, every experience, at every stage of life count. Clear challenges, however, will be presented from the massive collection of personal data, from the ethical, technological and confidentiality standpoint. There would be a dire need for legislative tools capable of managing the multifaceted nature of data and its value to each person's life – very much in line with Art. 22 of the GDPR on "automated individual decision making, including profiling" but of greater scope. From the technological standpoint, this wealth of strategic, long-term value cannot reside and transit in anything but a national and sovereign infrastructure that would need to be transversal across the technology stratum, including new access paradigms like 6G (becoming a reality in 2030[144]), the new generation networks and radio access, and a national data cente, as part of each nation's strategic reserve as much as gold, oil, gas, grain and water. A clear sovereignty of data in this field may find its way up to ethics; and if that happens, how should we mediate between opacity of non-necessary

137 Johnson, R. W. & Mommaerts, C. (2011). *Age differences in job loss, job search, and reemployment* (p. 22, Table 10). Washington DC: The Urban Institute. Kletzer, L. G. (1998). Job displacement. *Journal of Economic Perspectives*, 12(1), 125. Couch, K. A. & Placzek, D. W. (2010). Earnings losses of displaced workers revisited. *The American Economic Review*, 100(1). An extensive literature review on the topic, in addition to valuable original analysis, is also in Quintini, G. & Venn, D. (2013). *Back to work: Re-employment, earnings and skill use after job displacement*. OECD.

138 Sherington, G. E. (1976). The 1918 Education Act: Origins, aims and development. *British Journal of Educational Studies*, 68–85.

139 Skillsfuture is a national movement to provide Singaporeans with the opportunities to develop their fullest potential throughout life, regardless of their starting points. Through this movement, the skills, passion and contributions of every individual will drive Singapore's next phase of development towards an advanced economy and inclusive society. No matter where participants are in life – schooling years, early career, mid-career or silver years – they will find a variety of resources to help attain mastery of skills. Skills mastery is more than having the right paper qualifications and being good at what you do currently; it is a mindset of continually striving towards greater excellence through knowledge, application and experience. The initiative has the support of Singapore Future Economy Council, education and training providers, employers and unions.

140 See *Opportunities*, p. 76, and *Digital's Cleaving Power*, p. 46.

141 Sparks, P. (2017, June). *The route to a trillion devices. The outlook for IoT investment to 2035*. ARM White Paper.

142 See *Dematerialized Work*, p. 64.

143 Stanford 2025. "Axis Flip". Retrieved from http://www.stanford2025.com/axis-flip.

144 Latva-aho, M. & Leppänen, K. (2019). Key drivers and research challenges for 6G ubiquitous wireless intelligence. *6G Research Visions* 1. University of Oulu. 6G Flagship (2020). White Paper on 6G Drivers and the UN SDGs. *6G Research Visions*, No. 2.

145 Dede, C. & Richards, J. (2020). *The 60-year curriculum: New models for lifelong learning in the digital economy.* New York: Routledge, Taylor & Francis Group.

146 Gratton, L. & Scott, A. (2016). *The 100-year life living and working in an age of longevity.* London: Bloomsbury.

147 Currently the responsibility seems to be on the employers' shoulder with the WARN Act (Worker Adjustment and Retraining Notification Act) a law that requires employers to provide advance notice and planning mechanisms to their workforce and communities, in the event of a qualified plant closing or mass layoff. The United States Department of Labor has set guidelines for employers to properly follow WARN requirements. Certain states have analogous state laws, referred to as "mini-WARN acts". See Busch, D. M. & Follansbee, E. (2020, 2 April). *The WARN Act and COVID-19: What are employers obligated to do?* Mintz. In Switzerland, the most innovative country in the world for the Global Innovation Index 2020, there is the obligation to make every reasonable effort to shorten your unemployment, but there is no notion of forced retraining. See Dutta, S., Lavin, B. & Wunsch-Vincent, S. (Eds). (2020). *Global Innovation Index 2020. Who will finance innovation?* (13th ed.). Cornell, INSEAD, WIPO, 2020. Swiss Confederation center of competence for patent, design and trade mark protection. *Global Innovation Index 2020 – Switzerland remains the most innovative country in the world.* IGE|IPI Press release, 3 Sep 2020. The public guidance to help the unemployed, published at https://arbeit.swiss, FAQ, question 4. Moreover, in a world moving in the Gig economy, there will be fewer and fewer employers willing to retrain those laid off (so much for the WARN Act), and thus retraining will become an individual responsibility.

data for companies and organizations, transparency for data for its producers and owners (the people), and the need for privacy and security throughout the entire platform? It is true as well that the next-generation workforce needs to be well prepared for a high-road, technologically augmented economy, that might regard some of these issues as something from the past. And companies are likely to be more willing to create such an economy if they are convinced that the country's educational infrastructure is doing all it can to produce a workforce that is constantly on the cutting edge and ready, willing and able to keep the new economy advancing. Thus, both parties can do their part to build a new social contract at work to empower this positive vision.

Enabling Laws may encompass allowing seniors to continue to work, adapting to the new paradigms of working, and learning, like with the 60-year curriculum[145] and the 100-year life,[146] and along the same lines, financial support for the unemployed willing to reorient their career, maybe through a substantial pivot towards a more future-proof industry or job. Another aspect where *Enabling Laws* will be expected to make an impact will be obsolescence prevention and lifelong learning. It could be envisioned through planning a legal responsibility to retrain in order to be entitled to unemployment insurance.[147] Lastly, a support action valorizing risk taking would grant more access to startup funding, accelerating the transit through the innovation funnel[148] – from seeds to unicorns.

Secondly, from the *Enabling Laws* angle, the issue of data and data collection will be something to be tackled more deeply than from a legislative perspective. It will be a matter addressing at free will in a sense, because what will this infrastructure make of individual choice? This could get to constitutional rights, morals, and even ethics. At the same time, it is not that far from what happens with profiling with streaming services or social networks. And not every part of it is bad. Profiling gives more relevant suggestions, fast-track objectives, and is a disruptive tool for empowering when it is used for the good of the person. Imagine the potential of a "Spotify for skilling" as the one imagined in *Digital's Cleaving Power*, combined with the unbelievable granularity and insight possible through the paradigm of quantified self. In all this "fog of more"[149] consisting in the overload of support, more options, more tools, more knowledge, more advice, and more requirements, but not always more actual results, we need to break the waves of uncertainty for an evolved body of laws and set a clear direction for where the laws should aim. It will need to develop and support the transformations incoming and their nonlinearity and plurality. Once again, the need for a new social contract is steadfast, bridging the need to encourage entrepreneurship to thrive in a growing Gig economy and the need to cover for the risks which a fully individualistic society carries, such as the disappearance of unions. The postwar social contract was built on a foundation of a mutually supportive set of economic and political conditions. Large companies, on the one side, had the power to influence buying habits and set prices high enough to ensure satisfactory profits. Strong labor unions, on the other side, were able to secure consistently higher pay and better benefits for their members and for other workers. However, as technology and social fabric interweave in unexpected and surprising ways, there is no doubt we will be able to shape a social security as powerful, even in a radically different scenario driven by the Gig economy.

148 Du Preez, N. D. & Louw, L. A. (2008). *Framework for managing the innovation process*. In PICMET'08-2008 Portland International Conference on Management of Engineering & Technology, pp. 546-558. IEEE. Flynn, M., Dooley, L., O'Sullivan, D. & Cormican, K. (2003). *Idea management for organisational innovation*. *International Journal of Innovation Management*, 7(04), 417–442.

149 From the original Council on CyberSecurity Annual 2014 Report: "Overload of defensive support: More options, more tools, more knowledge, more advice, and more requirements, but not always more security". See also Sager, T. (2014). *The "fog of more": A cybersecurity community challenge*. RSA Conference.

10. New Value Schemes

Disruption will not spare the way we frame reality from our inner self, where values (and, thus, ethics) are residing. New generations will follow value schemes and networks broader and widely different from what we can imagine. Generation Z and the following Generation Alpha will bring a responsible approach to our planet, its resources, and climate. Their sensitivity to climate matters will be rooted in their habits and in the way they will make sense of the world. Ideas like the blue economy,[150] decarbonization, and circular economy will be at the top of their agenda. A movement of increasing nature consciousness, coupled with *Dematerialized Work*, *Digital's Cleaving Power*, and *More, Faster*, will bring any kind of work around the country and across countries. With technology allowing for remote work, research will happen everywhere in the country, moving past the paradigm of centralized research centers.[151] With such a strong need to go back to the roots, back to nature, supported by the technology to work remotely, and actually letting workers work remotely, we will go from the anonymity of big city centers to a new sense of community in the countryside. This will mean for HR that jobs will not have location at a premium anymore (surpassing the old saying "location, location, location"), instead employees will focus on content, purpose, and possibility of remotization. The H "half" of HR will be empowered the most.

Economic growth will not mean anymore environmental degradation – these two concepts will land to a definitive decoupling in the Thirties.

Some of the *New Value Schemes* will emerge from within the society and will be impacting the labor market and employers. Keywords belonging to these will be search for purpose, aim for positive impact, flexibility, diversity. Others will be guided – when not outright imposed on the world of work – by external forces, such as governmental, political, national or international. An example here is the 17 Sustainability Development Goals (SDGs).[152]

In 2030 a good share of the SDGs should have been realistically reached or on a good track to be reached in the next 5–10 years. Knowledge and awareness of the United Nations' 2030 Agenda for Sustainable Development is not quite what you could call widespread, with just over 1 in 10 Europeans knowing what SDGs are[153] and a global awareness of just the 26%.[154]

So, here is what a world on SDGs will look like.[155] In 2030, extreme poverty will have been eradicated for all people everywhere, reducing at least by half the proportion of men, women and children of all ages living in poverty in all its dimensions. The poor and the vulnerable will have ensured equal rights to economic resources, access to basic services, ownership and control over land, natural resources, appropriate new technology and financial services. Hunger will be on a strong track towards disappearance, and access by all people to safe, nutritious and sufficient food all year round will be ensured. Malnutrition will be a thing of the past, and the agricultural productivity and incomes of small-scale food producers will be double. There will be sustainable and resilient food ecosystems, adaptable to climate change and extreme weather; genetic diversity will have been safeguarded and preserved.

By 2030, epidemics of AIDS, tuberculosis, malaria and tropical diseases, will be finally overcome, with fights against other endemics underway. Mortality from diseases will drop by a third, the number of injuries from road traffic will be halved, the number of illnesses from pollution will be reduced steeply as well, and humankind will achieve universal access to sexual healthcare and universal health coverage. All girls and boys will be able to complete free and quality primary and secondary education, with equal access to quality early childhood development and quality tertiary education. Facilities and measures will have been put in place to give a substantial share of youth and adults relevant skills, e.g. technical and vocational skills, for employment and entrepreneurship. On the other hand, unpaid care and domestic work will have been recognized and valued, ensuring women's full and effective participation and equal opportunities for leadership at all levels. Still on the women's side, as stated above, by 2030, universal access to sexual health and rights will be ensured. There has been and still will be reforms to give women equal rights to economic resources and to enhance the use of enabling technologies for empowerment of women. Policies will be renewed, adopted and strengthened.

There will be universal and equitable access to safe and affordable drinking water for all, with adequate and equitable sanitation and hygiene. Water quality will be improved by reducing pollution, halving untreated wastewater, and increasing recycling and safe reuse globally. We will fight water scarcity through increased water-use efficiency and a sustainable ensured supply of freshwater through integrated water resources management that will also enable the protection of water-related ecosystems. Universal access to affordable, reliable and modern energy services will be a reality, as will a substantial increase of the share of renewable energy in the global energy mix. We will assist in doubling the global rate of improvement in energy efficiency, promoted through investments in energy infrastructure and clean energy technology, expanded infrastructure and upgraded technology for supplying modern and sustainable energy services for all. The per capita economic growth will be supported for a steady increase, and up at least 7% GDP in the least developed countries. Economic productivity will reach all-time highs through diversification, technological upgrading and innovation, and promotion of development-oriented policies accordingly, strengthening domestic access to banking and finance. Economic growth will not mean anymore environmental degradation – these two concepts will land to a definitive decoupling in the Thirties.

There will be a hard core from degrowth and collapsology versus industrial ecology and technology optimists.

Economic development and human well-being will receive great support through the development of quality, reliable, sustainable and resilient infrastructure. Inclusive and sustainable industry will see its share of employment and GDP rise, and SMEs will enjoy increased access to credit and integration with the large industries' ecosystem. By 2030, there will be a radical upgrade of infrastructures with "green" technologies, as a result of actions aimed at enhancing scientific research, upgrading

150 Pauli, G. (2012). *The blue economy: 10 jahre – 100 innovationen – 100 millionen jobs.* Berlin: Konvergenta.
151 This is already happening at EPFL scattered throughout the country until up the mountains). EPFL has 5 campuses – one of which in Lausanne – with all their specificities. For instance, Neuchâtel area is strong for microtechnique industry – so that is the field of research. One is in the Canton of Valais, close to the Alps, working on energy but also health and environment. For a complete description, please see https://www.epfl.ch/about/campus/.
152 United Nations (2015). *Transforming our world: The 2030 agenda for sustainable development.*
153 OECD Development Communication Network (DevCom) (2017, June). *What people know and think about the Sustainable Development Goals. Selected findings from public opinion surveys.*
154 Tedeneke, A. (2019, 23 September). *Global survey shows 74% are aware of the Sustainable Development Goals.* Press release. Data presented in the release, however – from a survey Ipsos conducted for the World Economic Forum – actually show that 74% globally of respondents were unaware of the SDGs, with answers being either "not very familiar", or "have heard of them, know nothing about them", or "have not heard of them". The Authors have reached out to WEF for a correction of the title.

technologies, increasing workers and spending in innovation and R&D. There will be an increase in financial and technological support, Research, Development & Innovation of domestic technology and universal, affordable access to the Internet. By 2030 we will achieve and sustain income growth of the bottom

By 2030 we will have reached the commitment, the capacity, and the capital for mobilizing $100B annually for climate.

40% of the population (accounting to roughly 4 billion people), empowering and promoting the social, economic and political inclusion of all, ensuring equal opportunity, reducing inequalities of outcome, and adopting fiscal and social protection policies. Orderly, safe, regular and responsible migration and mobility will be welcomed, facilitated, and managed.

Housing and basic services will be another field of vast advancements. Access for all to adequate, safe, affordable, accessible, inclusive and sustainable housing and basic services, transport systems, and urbanization will be ensured. Humankind will reduce the environmental impact of cities and provide universal access to green spaces, supporting positive links between urban and rural areas, and increasing adaptation to climate change and disaster resilience. Speaking of resources, we will achieve sustainable management and efficient use of natural resources, we will reduce per capita global food waste including postharvest losses, as well as an environmentally sound generation

and management of waste through prevention, reduction, recycling and reuse. Sustainability will be long integrated into product lifecycle, and sustainable practices will be commonplace. This will also bring the rationalization of inefficient fossil-fuel subsidies that encourage wasteful consumption. This will be part of a broader urgent action to combat climate change and its impacts, through resolutions that in 2030 will be widespread and strongly supported by policy, technology, organizations, and standards. This will strengthen resilience and adaptive capacity to climate-related hazards and natural disasters in all countries, integrating climate change measures into national policies, strategies and planning, and improving education, awareness-raising and human and institutional capacity on climate change mitigation, adaptation, impact reduction and early warning. By 2030 we will have reached the commitment, the capacity, and the capital for mobilizing $100B annually for climate from all sources – giving full operationalization to the Green Climate Fund.[156]

Marine, terrestrial and human ecosystems will enjoy an unprecedented level of harmony and abundance. Oceans, seas and marine resources will be conserved and used for sustainable development in a nurturing way. Terrestrial ecosystems will be protected, restored, and used sustainably. Forests will be managed for sustainable development, and humankind will combat desertification, halt and reverse land degradation, and halt biodiversity loss. The benefits of genetic resources will be valued, promoted, and shared fairly, alongside the integration of ecosystem and biodiversity values into national and local planning, development, and strategies. Humankind will have acted for its own ecosystem, promoting peaceful and inclusive

155 United Nations. *Ibid.*
156 Green Climate Fund – GCF is a unique global platform to respond to climate change by investing in low-emission and climate-resilient development. GCF was established by 194 governments to limit or reduce greenhouse gas (GHG) emissions in developing countries, and to help vulnerable societies adapt to the unavoidable impacts of climate change. See https://www.greenclimate.fund/.
157 Degrowth is an idea that critiques the global capitalist system which pursues growth at all costs, causing human exploitation and environmental destruction. The degrowth movement of activists and researchers advocates for societies that prioritize social and ecological well-being instead of corporate profits, over-production and excess consumption. See for instance Kallis, G. et al. (2020). *The case for degrowth.* Polity Press.
158 Collapsology is a neologism used to designate the risks of collapse of our industrial civilization within our current lifetime. The word has been coined and brought to the attention of the general public in the essay: Servigne, P., Stevens, R., & Brown, A. (2020). *How everything can collapse: A manual for our times.* Cambridge, UK: Polity.
159 Wittgenstein, L. (1921). *Tractatus logico philosophicus.* New York, NY: Dover Publications.
160 See *More, Faster,* p. 42; and *AI & Humans,* p. 70.
161 Under the guise of *More, Faster,* p. 51; *Digital's Cleaving Power,* page 2; and *AI & Humans,* p. 79.
162 See *Aspiration & Life Design,* p. 108.
163 See *Centaurs & Knights,* p. 58; and *Transgenerational Bridging,* p. 142.
164 See *More, Faster,* p. 42.
165 See *Dematerialized Work,* p. 64; and *Digital's Cleaving Power,* p. 46.
166 See *Aspiration & Life Design,* p. 108.
167 See *Transgenerational Bridging,* p. 142.
168 See *Centaurs & Knights,* p. 58; *Trust,* p. 54; and *Community,* p. 50.
169 Dator, J. (2019). What Futures studies is, and is not. In J. Dator, *A Noticer in Time.* Anticipation Science 5 (3–5). Cham: Springer

societies for sustainable development, providing access to justice for all, and building effective, accountable and inclusive institutions at all levels. We will develop effective, accountable and transparent institutions at all levels, provide legal identity for all and broaden and strengthen the participation in global governance. This is the world SDGs are made to reach.

In this turbulent and uncertain landscape, Human Resources will be seen as the glue that crosses the organization systemically and enables holistic thinking.

Despite the incalculable progress made by humanity in a world of SDGs, there will be a hard core from degrowth[157] and collapsology[158] versus industrial ecology and technology optimists.

Conversely, bearing in mind that as AI continually evolves and is a compute-intensive endeavor, research in energy efficient AI or in new compute architecture will make it more "green" and will bear a differential value for organizations putting them forward. Vocabulary will be once again expanded and looked at with renewed interest, à la Wittgenstein.[159] Conversation around human resources will pivot to "People" and human "Capital", giving them identity, value, and recognition – moving past the "Resources" that draw upon a "Baby Boomer" mindset of earth resources and their mining and exploitation. The focus will instead be on the attention dedicated to workers, to public actions, to initiatives of corporate workforce responsibility, and to work–life balance.

HR will act as a capstone to this arch: it will be the nexus of social integration, diversity and care, present all-round for their people's mental and general well-being with an empowering eye, asking themselves and the company what more could they be doing. This aspect will be a cornerstone of expectations from newer generations, that will not be pardoning on this aspect. The rate of change and uncertainty brought by technology and its socio-technological implications[160] will knock down the 3-stage life model framing working life until the beginning of the 21st century, and job security in the workplace will vanish. The digital dimension will enable[161] the Gig economy to grow and will allow the loyalty towards employers to fade out. In this redefined labor market with reshuffled rules, new contracts will need to be established between employees and employers – moving towards a paradigm of, respectively, workforce and customer. We will assist to a shift in values; whereas loyalty was offered for security, in the Thirties engagement will be exchanged for employability. Employees will expect to be onboarded on experience journeys, to develop insights on their current placement and their life trajectory.[162] Conversely, we will see rising a new kind of branch to manage risks linked to old age pertaining work, interaction, seniority, and how to structure best a sort of "recovery net" to have the least loss of experience at the moment of retirement or exit – through mentoring paths,[163] or even brain uploads.[164] In this turbulent and uncertain landscape, HR will be seen as the glue that crosses the organization systemically and enables holistic thinking.

Dematerialized and digitally distributed work[165] will affect social ties, thus creating a growing need for new human connections either by rethinking workflows and structures[166] or by making new links possible.[167] With the rise of technology and social networks,[168] the very concept of information and trust will have shifted and the new holders of the "truth" will be the influencers – increasingly trusted and sought after for their advice on everything and anything. The value of human contact and the individual, rather than the group, will be on the rise.

Generation Z and the following Generation Alpha will bring a responsible approach to our planet, its resources, and climate.

Another aspect of new values the future workforce will be scrutinizing is about fairness and equity. Procedures that are transparent, comprehensible, lean, flexible and recognized will be an asset for any future organization trying to attract the best talent. A broader distribution of earnings will give a message of special attention to merit and achievements, without leaving the human element out. And with Data Oceans incoming, infrastructure ownership will be a significant plus: being able to guarantee that everything happening within the physical and digital boundaries of the organization will in some cases be priceless. As humans produce data, data shape humans through human access to the information contained in them. Paraphrasing Dator's Third Law of Future,[169] humans produce data and therefore data produce humans, up to the point of imagining that access to network will be a fundamental right in 2030 – not only because of access to Data Oceans and the algorithm economy, but mainly because network means, and will increasingly mean, presence and representation.

22 NEW HR DISCIPLINES

Towards the 22nd century

Influenced by one or many Traits of Futures as introduced previously, the 22 Disciplines described in this volume are variants of today's HR work or radically new roles. They should be regarded as help for assessing the organizations' current level of future-readiness, a potential lever to allow for the organization to evolve, and as a guide for HR leaders to prepare and anticipate for change.

While some of the concepts and disciplines presented in this volume may seem futuristic or even science-fiction-like, others already exist today or will in the very near future.

Futures may come in many guises and may develop differently in different places, and at different paces.

Regardless of the level of future-readiness of organizations, their size or type of industry, it is essential for them to keep anticipating, dreaming, imagining and always staying one step ahead.

HR leaders are the cornerstone to navigate the future and to set a solid foundation for organizations to thrive towards the 22nd century. We need to empower them.

Cross-correlation analysis

The 22 Disciplines presented hereafter have a solid anchoring in the current observable 10 Traits of Futures. The traits, although distinct from one another, are very much intertwined in the impact they have on the world of work. The 22 Disciplines designed find ground and meaning in many of them as clearly visualized by this chord diagram.

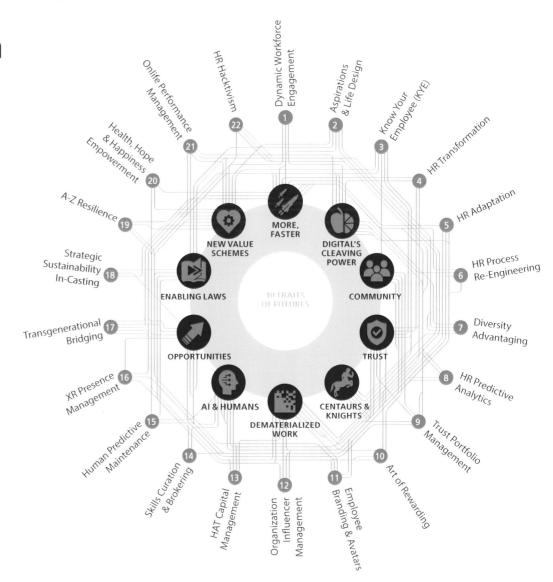

From today
to tomorrow

Although the 10 Traits of Futures could have a seismic impact on the world of HR, changes will most likely happen incrementally. Current and traditional disciplines will evolve to meet the new needs of the organization at a pace dictated by both the market needs and the organizations' assessment of potential impact and the related costs of upgrading disciplines.

Most of the new 22 Disciplines proposed in this volume can be described as evolving from selected traditional HR disciplines. Considering that HR structures and activities are extremely diverse and depend on organizations' size, purpose or industries, we relied on O*NET, an online service developed for the US Department of Labor, for information on capability requirements in profiles of standard jobs. For the sake of clarity and simplicity, we have selected ten traditional HR disciplines extracted and reorganized from the O*NET database. The database relies on a national center for development which is involved in a continual data collection process aimed at identifying and maintaining up-to-date information on the characteristics of workers and jobs[170] – *as they are today* and not particularly as they will or should be tomorrow – thus giving a good image of HR as currently organized.

> *The domain in which HR tends to be the weakest is in understanding and applying technology to build HR.*
>
> David Ulrich, *HR from the Outside In:*
> *Six Competencies for the Future of Human Resources*

170 Tsacoumis, S. & Willson, S. (2010). *O*NET analyst occupational skill*
     ratings: Procedures. Human Resources Research Organization.
171 *Ibid.*

TRADITIONAL OVERARCHING HR DISCIPLINES AS DESCRIBED IN O*NET[171]

22 NEW & GROWING HR DISCIPLINES

HR management & operations

- Serve as a link between management and employees by handling questions, interpreting and administering contracts, and helping resolve work-related problems.
- Plan, direct, supervise, and coordinate work activities of subordinates and staff relating to employment, compensation, labor relations, and employee relations.
- Prepare and follow budgets for personnel operations.

1 Dynamic Workforce Engagement

5 HR Adaptation   **6** HR Process Re-Engineering

12 Organization Influencer Management

22 HR Hacktivism   **20** Health, Hope & Happiness Empowerment

HR strategy

- Study legislation, arbitration decisions, and collective bargaining contracts to assess industry trends.

4 HR Transformation

5 HR Adaptation

18 Strategic Sustainability In-Casting

19 A–Z Resilience

HR recruiting & planning

- Identify staff vacancies and recruit, interview, and select applicants.
- Prepare personnel forecast to project employment needs.
- Allocate human resources, ensuring appropriate matches between personnel.
- Oversee the evaluation, classification, and rating of occupations and job positions.
- Plan and conduct new employee orientation to foster positive attitudes towards organizational objectives.
- Develop, administer, and evaluate applicant tests.
- Outplacement.

3 Know Your Employee (KYE)

14 Skills Curation & Brokering

TRADITIONAL OVERARCHING HR DISCIPLINES AS DESCRIBED IN O*NET[171]

22 NEW & GROWING HR DISCIPLINES

Compensation & benefits

- Analyze and modify compensation and benefits policies to establish competitive programs and ensure compliance with legal requirements.
- Administer compensation, benefits, and performance management systems, and safety and recreation programs.

(10) Art of Rewarding

HR analytics

- Conduct exit interviews to identify reasons for employee termination.
- Maintain records and compile statistical reports concerning personnel-related data such as hires, transfers, performance appraisals, and absenteeism rates.

(3) Know Your Employee (KYE)

(8) HR Predictive Analytics

(14) Skills Curation & Brokering

Learning & development, evaluations

- Plan, organize, direct, control, or coordinate the personnel, training, or labor relations activities of an organization.
- Analyze training needs to design employee development, language training, and health and safety programs.

(3) Know Your Employee (KYE)

(14) Skills Curation & Brokering

(15) Human Predictive Maintenance

(19) A–Z Resilience

(21) Onlife Performance Management

HR innovation

- Develop or administer special projects in areas such as pay equity, savings bond programs, day care, and employee awards.

(4) HR Transformation

(6) HR Process Re-Engineering

(8) Diversity Advantaging

(19) A–Z Resilience

TRADITIONAL OVERARCHING HR DISCIPLINES AS DESCRIBED IN O*NET[171]

22 NEW & GROWING HR DISCIPLINES

HR risks & complaints

- Analyze statistical data and reports to identify and determine causes of personnel problems and develop recommendations for improvement of organization's personnel policies and practices.
- Investigate and report on industrial accidents for insurance carriers.
- Perform difficult staffing duties, including dealing with understaffing, refereeing disputes, firing employees, and administering disciplinary procedures.
- Conduct exit interviews to identify reasons for employee termination.
- Advise managers on organizational policy matters, such as equal employment opportunity and sexual harassment, and recommend needed changes.

(1) Dynamic Workforce Engagement

(20) Health, Hope & Happiness Empowerment

HR marketing

- Provide current and prospective employees with information about policies, job duties, working conditions, wages, opportunities for promotion, and employee benefits.

(7) Diversity Advantaging   (11) Employee Branding & Avatars

(18) Strategic Sustainability In-Casting

(20) Health, Hope & Happiness Empowerment

HR law & unions

- Represent organization at personnel-related hearings and investigations.
- Negotiate bargaining agreements and help interpret labor contracts.

(7) Diversity Advantaging   (12) Organization Influencer Management

(16) XR Presence Management   (10) Art of Rewarding

(21) Onlife Performance Management

NEW

(2) Aspirations & Life Design   (9) Trust Portfolio Management

(13) HAT Capital Management   (17) Transgenerational Bridging

At a glance

Influenced by the Traits of Futures, existing traditional HR disciplines will evolve, and new focus areas will emerge. While some should be urgently addressed, others represent the opportunity to rapidly gain a competitive advantage attracting and retaining talents, and some could be considered necessary for organizations willing to prepare for low-probability, high-risk contingencies.

HR leadership will decide when and how to up their game based on their organization's realities and constraints. Among the boundary conditions influencing the space of solutions and actions here, there is of course the value HR leadership sees in integrating all, a class of, or just singled out disciplines. The following graphic shall offer a good understanding of the potential impact and costs linked with setting up specific new disciplines within HR.

STATUS QUO
While many existing HR disciplines will remain highly relevant and fundamental, the current pace of change and disruptions call for an evolution of HR identity and HR action. That is why this quadrant is empty; we simply cannot keep going with the flow pretending this is not happening to the organization we are in, and that we are doing great anyway. Traditional HR disciplines will have to evolve – en masse.

ACT NOW
All new HR disciplines that are listed in this quadrant are ripe, and will become mainstream at the speed of relevance. If HR departments do not take action and integrate these disciplines, they will lose the momentum and literally move backwards compared to other market players.

GAIN THE EDGE

It is key to ensure that organizations take advantage of the forces acting upon the labor market, rather than resisting them. It is vital to gain an edge on the competition, and attract, retain and nurture the best talents. We are entering a war for talents, and today is the best day for HR to start positioning itself as a strategic pivotal function.

PREPARE FOR THE UNTHINKABLE

To anticipate future shocks, organizations need to think beyond the plausible, and HR function must initiate and nurture this exponential and sometimes divergent thinking within its ranks and beyond. The lack of almost any disciplines fitting the bottom right corner is a promising way ahead for this endeavor. It is not a shortcoming of the groupwork, but instead a design choice due to the various constraints of the project. It confirms the need to explore the fringe futures lying at the far boundary of Possible futures in the Futures Cone, so as to be able to give a meaningful answer to the new kind of questions treasured in that quadrant.

Before any major investment to reorganize or reskill an organization or part of an organization, be it in time or money, leaders like to assess potentialities, state of the art and feasibility. To that effect, we have created a unique scale: the REAL Scale. The REAL Scale value is a grade, estimated via experts' assessments, and expressed visually through the size of a red circle for each discipline. It gives an instant visual cue as to the current global readiness level of the discipline. It indicates the level of the forces in place today for a discipline to start developing, scale up and become mainstream. The REAL grade is computed using 4 sub-criteria:

- *Real awareness* – what level of awareness already exists in society/organizations with regards to this new discipline?

- *Enabling ecosystem* – will the current ecosystem allow for this discipline to grow and become mainstream?

- *Available technologies* – does this discipline require specific technologies, and if yes, is this technology ready and available?

- *Laid-out action* – can we already see organizations deploying such disciplines? Are the skills to perform them already taught?

22 NEW & GROWING HR DISCIPLINES

1. Dynamic Workforce Engagement
2. Aspirations & Life Design
3. Know Your Employee (KYE)
4. HR Transformation
5. HR Adaptation
6. HR Process Re-Engineering
7. Diversity Advantaging
8. HR Predictive Analytics
9. Trust Portfolio Management
10. Art of Rewarding
11. Employee Branding & Avatars
12. Organization Influencer Management
13. HAT Capital Management
14. Skills Curation & Brokering
15. Human Predictive Maintenance
16. XR Presence Management
17. Transgenerational Bridging
18. Strategic Sustainability In-Casting
19. A–Z Resilience
20. Health, Hope & Happiness Empowerment
21. Onlife Performance Management
22. HR Hacktivism

REAL SCALE

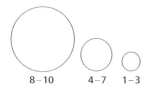

8–10   4–7   1–3

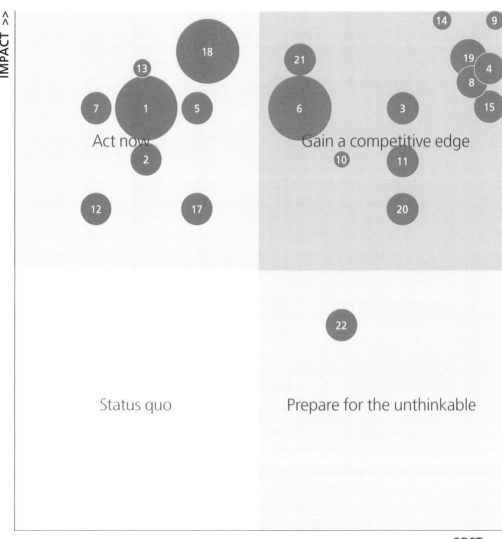

THE NEW HR DISCIPLINES

Purpose
Although all 22 new Disciplines serve the advancement of the overall HR function, they each have a distinct purpose that defines them.

Evolves from
New disciplines can be seen as an evolution from various existing disciplines or domains, such as the following ones inspired by O*NET.

Traits of Futures
The 10 Traits of Futures are overarching themes and trends impacting the evolution of the HR function. Each of the 22 new Disciplines emerges from one or several Traits of Futures.

Quote
From the top of the hierarchy to business experts, from technical scientists to social scientists, our HR Futures 2030 foresight workshop involved individuals who all held a key to envision new futures of the HR function. We were happy to give them the opportunity to comment on each.

0. Discipline Specimen

PURPOSE
Text

EVOLVES FROM
List of traditional disciplines
- HR management & operations
- HR strategy
- HR recruiting & planning
- Compensation & benefits
- HR analytics
- Learning & development, evaluations
- HR innovation
- HR risks & complaints
- HR marketing
- HR law & unions

TRAITS OF FUTURES
List of traits of futures

Quote by:
First Name Last Name
Organization/Institution
Position

MYTHOLOGY

Demigod   Centaur   Knight

Minotaur   Monk

AT A GLANCE   Impact: X/10
                         Costs: X/10

Impact >>

Costs >>

We gave a voice to the Designers & Dreamers who took part in the foresight event to comment on each discipline with a specific quote.

REAL SCALE

Real awareness

Enabling ecosystem

Available technologies

Laid-out action

Total: X/10

Mythology
New disciplines can be better suited for specific individuals with particular personality traits, preferences and values as described earlier under mythological figures. This should help the reader relate to one or another discipline for ulterior further re-/upskilling actions.

At a glance
This graph indicates the pertinence of investigating and upskilling into new HR disciplines according to their potential impact and cost for your organization.

Real scale
It analyzes and aggregates the awareness of each discipline, the existing ecosystem for growth, the current technology readiness level, as well as the existing actions already laid out in the market in 2020.

Signals and trends

The emergence of new disciplines as perceived by the group and based on the traits of the future are supported and confirmed by current weak (or strong) signals from the market, society and the environment.

Responsibilities

Under *responsibilities* we propose selected actions which should serve the general purpose of the discipline. This list of suggestions is by no means an exhaustive list, but a guideline.

SIGNALS AND TRENDS

RESPONSIBILITY

1. Dynamic Workforce Engagement

PURPOSE
Keep employees motivated, committed and engaged with the organization in order to secure a competitive edge on human capital and mitigate turnover risks and consequent costs.

EVOLVES FROM
HR management & operations
HR risks & complaints

TRAITS OF FUTURES
1. More, Faster
2. Digital's Cleaving Power
10. New Value Schemes

MYTHOLOGY

Knight   Monk

AT A GLANCE   Impact: 8/10
                       Costs: 3/10

Act now

Impact >>

Costs >>

REAL SCALE

Real awareness

Enabling ecosystem

Available technologies

Laid-out action

Total: 8/10

Quote by:
CHRISTOPHE BARMAN
Loyco
Founder

As self-employment and the need for sense-driven careers will rise, corporations will have to engage employees by offering trust, autonomous work and purpose. Failing in that will make them lose the war for talents and disappear.

SIGNALS AND TRENDS

We ought not to buy into the narrative of the inevitable rise of the job-hopping millennial. Statistics from 2020 show that job-hopping was much higher in the 1980s.[172] However, new digital platforms, such as UpWork and Fiverr or Freelancer.com that enable the growth of the Gig economy, will inevitably draw employees out of the comfort of employment towards the liberty of self-employment. Organizations will have to fight for the right talents.

In parallel, although most employee-employer relationships operated on a mutual loyalty pact for decades, with tenure valued and representing security, the employee-employer relationship saw a paradigm shift in liability. With the rise of the shareholder concept, in which each person had to look out for their own best interests, the employer was no longer taking care of the employees' interests – employees now need to care for themselves.

Employee engagement is a way to meet both challenges. Although there are various definitions to "employee engagement", we shall consider the Gallup Organization's definition (2006) which states that *"engaged employees are those who work with a passion and feel a profound connection to their company, drive innovation and move the organization in forward direction."*

Besides bringing an undeniable positive outlook for the organizations, a higher level of engagement among employees will encourage effective communication, foster innovation, develop loyalty and ultimately bring along higher results.

Conversely, without employee engagement, employers can struggle to adapt themselves to the changing environment or retain the important members of staff that give a business its value.[173]

The importance of engagement has been captured by many organizations already, and startups have emerged to allow the uncovering of hidden drivers of engagement and scaling people enablement for forward-thinking companies.[174] However, although data-driven tools are very useful to foster engagement, employee engagement relies on whole company culture, being aligned from top to bottom.

RESPONSIBILITY

Model the company's core values and purpose to show how employees are each and together working towards a greater goal. Develop a feedback culture, conduct workforce engagement pulse surveys, and allow for company culture evolution to align to the employees' shifting needs. Ensure the rise of disciplines such as "Know Your Employee (KYE)" and "Aspirations & Life Design" to work at a more granular and individual engagement level improvement.

172 Tarki, A. & Malm, A. (2020, 16 March). Your employees are more loyal than you think. *Economics & Society.* Harvard Business Review.

173 Singh, Y. (2019). Employee engagement as a contemporary issue in HRM. In N. Sharma et al. (Eds.), *Management techniques for employee engagement in contemporary organizations* (pp. 20–45). IGI Global.

174 *Develop your people, scale your business.* See https://www.leapsome.com/.

2. Aspirations & Life Design

PURPOSE

With career transition being a painful crisis for both the employee and the employer, it is important to anticipate and ease changes within the organization and outside, to improve the employee experience before, during and after the employment contract, and thus improve the organization's brand and attractiveness.

EVOLVES FROM —

TRAITS OF FUTURES

1. More, Faster
5. Centaurs & Knights
6. Dematerialzed Work
9. Enabling Laws
10. New Value Schemes

MYTHOLOGY

Centaur · Knight · Monk

AT A GLANCE

Impact: 7/10
Costs: 3/10

Act now

Impact >>

Costs >>

REAL SCALE

Real awareness

Enabling ecosystem

Available technologies

Laid-out action

Total: 5/10

Quote by:
FRÉDÉRIC ROGER
AIR HR Global Solutions
CEO & Founder

The 21st century has disrupted the concept of employability and what defines it. Organizations now need to help employees be the architects of their own careers, offering coaching and education in exchange for high engagement and motivation.

SIGNALS AND TRENDS

In a world of work defined by growing blurred lines between private life and professional life, by evolving skills requirements, and by the end of the three-stage-life (study–work–retire), the psychological contract exchanging stability for security is giving way to new contracts based on the exchange of performance for a promise of increased employability and career guidance.[175]

In the era of the Gig economy, where career trajectories are now Z-shaped vis-à-vis linear, evolving into anxiety and insecurity for the former generation, the very concept of "employability" must be redesigned to fit the novel and unsaid rules of this new world of work. Although organizations have been offering transition support (such as outplacement or coaching) in various intensities or forms for a long time, the inherent motivations usually are to prevent risks related to legal or public opinion and have little to do with employees themselves.[176]

In this redefined scenario, an ideal employer has to strive to become a partner all along one's career – to adapt to *New Value Schemes*.

The HR function must integrate life and professional coaching and offer to manage the employee–employer relationship before, during and after their employment – and back. Whereas the cycle was formerly inherently one-dimensional, with a beginning (recruitment), an evolution, and an end (retirement/lay off), it has now transformed into a two-dimensional journey. The employee's path may come across the employer's space several times in various places or roles (trainee, employee, coach, independent consultant, alumni, etc.).

RESPONSIBILITY

Build organization-wide awareness on employees' profiles, needs and preferences to anticipate their potential internal trajectories and propose career mobility. Follow labor market evolutions in order to support employees' life trajectories, including guidelines for up-/reskilling. Create and run an alumni program to keep the relation alive. Extend employee experience from recruitment to termination and further.

175 Cadin L. (2005). Les cadres français ont-ils bouleversé leur modèle de carrière ?. *Actes de la journée no 10 du GDR Cadres*, CEVIPOF, pp. 45-57.
176 Roger F. & Hayot E. (2020). La transition de carrière au 21ème siècle. Master thesis, MAS "Human Systems Engineering". HEIGVD.

3. Know Your Employee (KYE)

PURPOSE
Anticipate employees' needs and nurture them, for effective retention and increased engagement. Employee intimacy brings enhanced familiarity with the organization's customers and thus improves business performance in both the short and long term.

EVOLVES FROM
HR recruiting & planning
HR analytics
Learning & development, evaluations

TRAITS OF FUTURES
3. Community
4. Trust
5. Centaurs & Knights
8. Opportunities
10. New Value Schemes

MYTHOLOGY

Centaur　　　Knight　　　Monk

AT A GLANCE

Impact: 8/10
Costs: 8/10

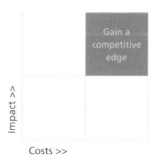

Gain a competitive edge

Impact >>

Costs >>

REAL SCALE

Real awareness

Enabling ecosystem

Available technologies

Laid-out action

Total: 6/10

Quote by:
CHRISTINE CHOIRAT
Swiss Data Science Center
EPFL & ETHZ
Chief Innovation Officer

 Data science has significantly matured over the last decade bringing unimaginable opportunities to understand one's environment, also in HR. Employees are your organization's greatest asset, you ought to know and valorize them!

SIGNALS AND TRENDS

Similarly to financial institutions which developed KYC (Know Your Customer) strategies in response to normative compliance and to ensure business sustainability, organizations and the HR function ought to develop a KYE (Know Your Employee) strategy to reach a higher level of employee intelligence and intimacy and to empower the design of more effective engagement strategies.

The foundation of "customer intimacy" is customer insight, based on what has come to be called customer intelligence. Consumer intelligence is the process of gathering, analyzing and exploiting rich sources of data about consumers, their activities and their environment[177] in order to build stronger and more effective customer relationships and thus allow for more informed strategic decision-making. The HR function should apply the same concept to employees and build employee intimacy, with employees being the link between the organization and the customer.

Yet, intimacy is not mere intelligence: it is a relationship. Building it requires more than amassing data, designing smart algorithms, or implementing novel analytical approaches. Intimacy requires moving beyond customer (or employee) intelligence, or even customer (employee) insight, towards true engagement.[178]

If engaging with *customers* at this deep level can pay off in significant ways – longer-term relationships, increased loyalty, and ultimately, sustained competitive performance – then it is reasonable to imagine that the same level of intimacy with employees can bring equal improvements to competitive performance.

It may require new processes and a different approach to human capital management, but employee-intimate companies could see a dramatic rise of employee productivity, performance, and value in the long term. Employee-intimate organizations look at the employee's lifetime value to the company, and not just at the value of a single transaction.[179]

RESPONSIBILITY

Develop an internal culture of genuine interest in individuals and the nurturing and fostering of real relationships. Run employee intimacy analytics, create real-time workforce dashboards to leverage operational data, and assess employee knowledge and relationships and measure their business impact. Employee intelligence leading to employee intimacy may include everything from pulse surveys, group discussions to text mining, or deep psychometric testing.

Know Your Employee (KYE) actions need to be applied at the micro level (the individual) and macro level (team or organization).[180]

177 Cooke, A. D. J. & Zubcsek, P. (2017). The connected consumer: Connected devices and the evolution of customer intelligence. *Journal of the Association for Consumer Research*, 2(2), 164–178.

178 Gobble, M.M. (2015). From customer intelligence to customer intimacy. *Research Technology Management*, 58(6), 56–60.

179 Borg, M. B., Brenner, G. H. & Berry, D. (2015). 5 benefits of corporate intimacy: Bringing the power of the acceptance of ourselves and others into the workplace. *Psychology Today*.

180 Habryn, F. (2012). *Customer intimacy analytics. Leveraging operational data to assess customer knowledge and relationships and to measure their business impact.* KIT Scientific Publishing. Karlsruher Institut für Technologie.

4. HR Transformation

PURPOSE
Propose, lead and manage fundamental changes within HR including its purpose, organization and processes to lead and support radical new aspects of the organization.

EVOLVES FROM
HR strategy
HR innovation

TRAITS OF FUTURES
1. More, Faster
2. Digital's Cleaving Power
4. Trust
7. AI & Humans

MYTHOLOGY

Demigod   Centaur

AT A GLANCE   Impact: 9/10
                        Costs: 10/10

Gain a competitive edge

Impact >>

Costs >>

REAL SCALE

Real awareness

Enabling ecosystem

Available technologies

Laid-out action

Total: 6/10

Quote by:
BENJAMIN MUELLER
UNIL | HEC Lausanne
Associate Professor

True HR transformation relies on anticipating what a world fully leveraging digital innovations will look like. Simply extrapolating the status quo just reinvents the present, but fails to imagine and shape the future.

SIGNALS AND TRENDS

It is one thing to describe, optimize and model processes based on existing methodologies to understand and improve a system's performance. It is another to use creative or disruptive thinking to imagine new ways of delivering a service/a task – and question the very pertinence of this service/task – in a world disrupted by data flows, major societal changes, and *New Value Schemes*.

To maintain their competitiveness in a faster world, crowded and even cluttered with data, with access to growing and democratized disruptive technologies, organizations will need to undertake a two-horizon approach. On the one hand, the short-term adaptation of their operations and processes exploit the novel opportunities given by technological forces in a new world, and the subsequent programmatic (re-)training of their workforce – which is the central topic of the other Discipline of this duo, HR Adaptation. On the other hand, the practice of long-term thinking, to not only react *ex post* to the changes happening in the world, but to anticipate them, and plan *ex ante*. This might even lead to changing the organizational geometry, its assets, and the forces it can exert on the environment to amplify weak signals. This enhancement of the ripples surfacing in the present day is instrumental to decision-makers' agency in driving the trajectory to the organization's desired future or the endstate sought-after. An example of this principle is conciliating the opposing organizational imperatives of ambidextrous organizations[181] in a fluid structure that has a permeable boundary across the two identities, to magnify on and exploit readily weak signals appearing in the organization's area of regard.

HR Transformation is the long-term expansionary force in Human Resources. This is a meta and very strategic function where HR reflects upon its own existence and pertinence, and reinvents itself in the light of the many changes brought upon by the Fourth Industrial Revolution. This might even redefine the very purpose of HR in certain organizations.

In times of rapid evolutions and seismic changes in the world of work, HR has the responsibility to become a fundamental "revolution force" of the organization, starting with its own transformation.

RESPONSIBILITY

Manage all the aspects about novelties and wild cards flowing into the working structure of the organization. Go beyond knowing the business towards a strategic partner to top-level leadership. Anticipate business trends and evolutions and rethink HR practices accordingly. Master and drive the processes of individual and institutional change.[182]

181 Tushman, M. L. & O'Reilly III, C. A. (2006). Ambidextrous organizations: Managing evolutionary and revolutionary change. *California Management Review*, 38(4).

182 Ulrich, D. (2016). HR at a crossroads. *Asia Pacific Journal of Human Resources*, 54, 148–164.

5. HR Adaptation

PURPOSE
Empower the execution of the long-term organizational strategy in the short-term. Act as the "glue" for all the facets of the organization's strategy to design the best organizational structure for it.

EVOLVES FROM
HR management & operations
HR strategy

TRAITS OF FUTURES
1. More, Faster
6. Dematerialzed Work
7. AI & Humans
8. Opportunities

MYTHOLOGY

Knight   Minotaur

AT A GLANCE   Impact: 8/10
                             Costs: 4/10

Act now

Impact >>

Costs >>

REAL SCALE

Real awareness

Enabling ecosystem

Available technologies

Laid-out action

Total: 7/10

Quote by:
JUDITH KONERMANN
Philip Morris International
*Global Head of Strategic
Workforce Planning*

Technology forces us to redesign our jobs and the way we work. HR has to take the exercise one step further and continuously redefine work and processes to ensure adaptability in an ever-changing environment.

SIGNALS AND TRENDS

While keeping the organization's aim and ambition straight over the horizon, at the long term, the initial steps to be taken need to be executed in the "here and now". Thus, the core topic of HR Adaptation is the short-term adaptation of the organization's operations and processes to exploit the novel opportunities given by technological forces in a new world, and the subsequent programmatic (re-)training of their workforce. This Discipline complements, supports, and brings more value to its long-term counterpart, HR Transformation, by designing, planning, and executing actions in the short term in keeping with the long-term trajectory.

Moreover, HR Adaptation is the internal *locus of control* of the organization where all the strategies – long-term, corporate, business, market and delivery – intertwine to create the best backdrop for the workforce to thrive. This Discipline is also in charge of integrating corporate strategy into the organization's structure, processes and profiles, taking corporate strategic objectives and flowing them down into the human dimension.

This might entail innovative, evolutionary ways of doing business and running operations, finding ways to experiment pioneering ideas from the other Discipline of HR Hacktivism to integrate a "fail fast or win big"[183] culture into the reactionary stalwart that HR is too often pictured to be, adaptively fine-tuning HR's geometry to support the organization's short-term execution of its long-term strategy.

RESPONSIBILITY

Move away from rigid employee structures and continuously adapt flexible teams of employees on the fly to new data and market conditions. Reimagine work processes thanks to emerging technological paradigms and social praxes to make the organization more efficient and help it reach its targets faster.

183 Schroeder, B. (2015). *Fail fast or win big: The start-up plan for starting now.* AMACOM.

6. HR Process Re-Engineering

PURPOSE
Adapt current HR operations to the evolved organizations, environment and exploit new automation and digitalization technologies to design and execute faster, leaner processes, flexible and adaptable, underpinning the resilience and the competitive edge of the organization.

EVOLVES FROM
HR management & operations
HR innovation

TRAITS OF FUTURES
1. More, Faster
2. Digital's Cleaving Power
7. AI & Humans
8. Opportunities

MYTHOLOGY

Knight

Minotaur

AT A GLANCE

Impact: 8/10
Costs: 6/10

Gain a competitive edge

Impact >>

Costs >>

REAL SCALE

Real awareness

Enabling ecosystem

Available technologies

Laid-out action

Total: 8/10

Quote by:
JÉRÔME RUDAZ
HR Vaud
President

As HR processes are becoming increasingly complex, organizations – big or small – ought to rely on the emerging and ripe technologies to ease, streamline and optimize work. Automatizing HR will allow us to concentrate more on the H of HR.

SIGNALS AND TRENDS

If the overall purpose of an organization and its existing functions does not drastically evolve in the short or even the medium term endogenously, organizations and functions will increasingly have to exploit new ways – especially automatized ways – of serving their own purpose to remain competitive.

Building on the "Automation Age", which saw its peak in the 1990s with Business Process Reengineering (BPR) thanks to advances in information technology, the "Cognitive Age"[184] is far more dramatic in its disruptive change than the previous transformation, as it ushers in entirely new and innovative ways of doing business and running operations. In the Cognitive Age, processes are reimagined to be more flexible, faster, and adaptable to the behaviors, preferences and needs of the workers at any given moment.

Given how complex and competitive the contemporary job landscape has become, technologies like augmented reality (AR) and VR can make a real difference, for example in recruitment, and an entertaining gamified experience will help attract the finest talent. Digitalizing recruitment processes can streamline systems, making work simpler and faster.[185]

While re-engineering processes of HR, decisions must be taken to either change or eliminate HR activities, if they do not add value. It is important to recognize that re-engineering the processes of HR means working in entirely different ways and often for the sole purpose of improving economic factors.[186]

Adapting HR to the organization's structure, processes and profile is rendered possible by the increase of available real-time data. Capturing enough data that describe and define the system will help the HR Leader update direction and reroute actions in real-time – recruitment, remuneration, education – much like a GPS does at each step of a trip, considering traffic, accidents, speed or weather.

This adaptative capability is being driven by real-time data rather than by sequences of steps listed, described and the automated.[187]

RESPONSIBILITY

Monitor HR technology trends, experiment and lead process reimagination with new designs, tools, technological upgrades, digitization, and training that can streamline processes and augment humans. Propose technological upgrades, lead digitizing processes, handle these responsibilities and train staff accordingly.

184 In the Information Age (circa 1950–2050), economy is dominated by knowledge workers using computers and other electronic devices in sectors like research, finance, consulting, information technology, and other services. Products are not physical anymore, and machine power is now substituting information and goods. Cfr. G. Rizzo, G. (2019). *Disruptive technologies in military affairs.* In F. Rugge (Ed.), *The global race for technological superiority.* Washington, DC: Brookings Institution and ISPI.

185 BasuMallick, Ch. (2018). How AR and VR are changing the recruitment process. *HR Technologist.*

186 Re-engineering HR delivery at IBM. (2002). *Human Resource Management International Digest,* 10(6), 9–12.

187 Wilson, H.J. & Daugherty, P.R. (2018). *Human + machine: reimagining work in the age of AI,* Boston, MA: Harvard Business Review Press.

The future is already here; it is just not very evenly distributed.

William Gibson
Novelist, science-fiction pioneer, coined the word "cyberspace" (1948–)

7. Diversity Advantaging

PURPOSE
Design your workforce – physical, virtual, nomadic, blended, hybrid – and set up work processes and values so as to exploit diversity as a concrete and unique competitive advantage.

EVOLVES FROM
HR innovation
HR marketing
HR law & unions

TRAITS OF FUTURES
1. More, Faster
5. Centaurs & Knights
9. Enabling Laws
10. New Value Schemes

MYTHOLOGY

Centaur   Knight   Monk

AT A GLANCE   Impact: 8/10
                        Costs: 2/10

Act now

Impact >>

Costs >>

REAL SCALE

Real awareness

Enabling ecosystem

Available technologies

Laid-out action

Total: 6/10

Quote by:
MIRAL HAMANI
Hewlett Packard Enterprise
Director & Associate

The world of work is complex. Humans are complex. It will really take all genders, cultures, ages, leadership styles and brain wiring to make sense of our environment and to empower organizations to thrive in the next decade.

SIGNALS AND TRENDS

Diversity has increasingly been regarded as a key topic in human capital management. It is time to leverage diversity, moving past the unsaid concept of "managing a quota", and handling public opinion to reach the exploitation of a concrete competitive advantage, both within the organization and outside, in the new lines delimiting the world of work (Gig economy, virtual workspaces, extended reality).

However, today diversity is too often still considered as just gender and race, and fails to encompass the underlying dynamics that can play a more decisive role within groups of people, such as diversity in attitudes, skills, knowledge and power. Diversity can provide advantages in the form of variety, new ideas and different knowledge sets.[188] Moreover, and especially pertinent in times of disruption, diversity allows for better environmental scanning and perception of complex environments.[189] Besides being a real asset in the running of operations, diversity – if exploited correctly and promoted – will help attract and retain talents. Organizations that signal diversity have a great way to interest and keep high potentials.[190]

But diversity for the sake of diversity, without team management for active inclusion, will not draw advantages; in fact, it may then be counterproductive. That is because shared knowledge is key in decision-making, and diverse teams, by definition, start out with less of it. But if you create conditions of trust that allow diverse team members to bring their unique perspectives and experiences to the table, you can expand the amount of knowledge your team can access – and create an unbeatable advantage. Ideal trust conditions will be even more necessary in a distributed workforce, which inherently proposed greater diversity in virtual teams. In virtual scattered worlds where different cultures and work methods collide, the risk of unhealthy racial and national stereotypes is high. It is then necessary to promote a common goal to foster identification in international virtual teams.[191] Diversity will also have to be encouraged and managed in cyberspace as an extended part of the world of work. Currently diversity is represented in cyberspace in a way that reflects the relative power of cultural economies across the globe.[192]

RESPONSIBILITY

Measure diversity and diversity management practices in organizations. Set SMART diversity objectives and adapt communication culture accordingly. Move away from "performance appraisals"[193] and focus on talent. Encourage dialog about diversity and find sponsors and champions who value difference and divergent thinking. Establish goals and accountability.

188 Klein, K. (2008). Diversity is not diversity is not diversity. *INSEAD Knowledge*.
189 Duchek, S., Raetze, S. & Scheuch, I. (2019). The role of diversity in organizational resilience: A theoretical framework. *Business Research*, 13, 387–423.
190 Arnett, R. (2018). How firms can do a better job of leveraging diversity. *Knowledge@Wharton*.
191 Au, Y. & Marks, A. (2012) Virtual teams are literally and metaphorically invisible: Forging identity in culturally diverse virtual teams. *Employee Relations*, 34(3), 217–287.
192 Jakubowicz, A. (2003). Democracy and new media: Ethnic diversity, "race" and the cultural political economy of cyberspace. In H. Jenkins & Thorburn, D. (Eds.), *Multiculturalism in Cyberia* (pp. 207–210). Cambridge Massachusetts: The MIT Press.
193 Performance appraisals were found to be a major source of discrimination. See for example Sharma, A. (2016). Managing diversity and equality in the workplace. T. Nisar (Ed.). *Cogent Business & Management*, 3(1).

8. HR Predictive Analytics

PURPOSE

Lead data-driven *anticipatory* perception over the workforce evolution, with more, real-time visibility. Capture, interpret and transform internal and external structured data into valuable insights (and foresight) for decision makers.

EVOLVES FROM

HR analytics

TRAITS OF FUTURES

1. More, Faster
2. Digital's Cleaving Power
7. AI & Humans
8. Opportunities

MYTHOLOGY

Centaur   Minotaur

AT A GLANCE

Impact: 9/10
Costs: 9/10

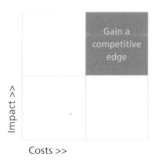

Gain a competitive edge

Impact >>

Costs >>

REAL SCALE

Real awareness

Enabling ecosystem

Available technologies

Laid-out action

Total: 7/10

Quote by:
OLIVIER VERSCHEURE
Swiss Data Science Center
EPFL & ETHZ
Director

Moving from data lakes to data oceans, from data on machines to data on humans, data science is a fantastic and global enhancer. Sensible exploitation of this massive amount of information using advanced analytics should become an integral part of HR.

SIGNALS AND TRENDS

People analytics has been a hot HR trend for years, even if it remains relatively basic in companies that did not integrate ERP systems. While many SMEs still rely on Excel sheets to manage their human capital data, the growing number of HR dashboard tools render the use of data increasingly accessible. More and more HR departments understand the power of instant, data-driven insights to boost business impact and consumer experience.[194]

On Deloitte's four levels of HR analytics maturity model[195] "1. operational reporting – descriptive", "2. advanced reporting – proactive", "3. predictive analytics", and "4. prescriptive analytics", most organizations stagnate at level 1.

Very few organizations have started, let alone mastered, the art of predictive or even prescriptive analytics.

However, the rapid advancement of intelligent technologies able to extract and analyze people data from within the organization to match it with open-source intelligence about people will represent a quantum leap for the potential of data insights in organizations, and will allow for better and more timely decisions on high-value human assets in the organizations.

Organizations are heavily investing in their data quality and analysis capabilities. Thanks to an advanced predictive analytics service, HR could run Organizational Network Analysis (ONA), launch "Organization's Internal Skills' Marketplaces" or use "Physiolitics" to monitor real-time employees' health and safety.

RESPONSIBILITY

Capture, structure, clean, and sanitize data acquired through the infrastructure. Serve as a key partner to drive various peripheral sub-roles or services to emerge such as ONA, skills-matching activities, etc.

194 Schmeichel, C. (2018). The future of people analytics: New horizons of intelligent HR consumer experience. *Digitalist Magazine*.
195 Bersin, J. (2017). *People analytics: Here with a vengeance*. Josh Bersin.

9. Trust Portfolio Management

PURPOSE
Build trust to allow for sustained productivity. If trust is the new gold, it will be scrutinized and monetized. Organizations must become data-driven on employees' trust.

EVOLVES FROM —

TRAITS OF FUTURES
2. Digital's Cleaving Power
3. Community
4. Trust
6. Dematerialzed Work
9. Enabling Laws
10. New Value Schemes

MYTHOLOGY

Demigod   Centaur   Monk

AT A GLANCE

Impact: 10/10
Costs: 6/10

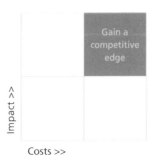

Gain a competitive edge

Impact >>

Costs >>

REAL SCALE

Real awareness

Enabling ecosystem

Available technologies

Laid-out action

Total: 3/10

Quote by:
BETTINA HUMMER
UNIL | School of Law
Professor

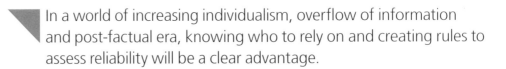

In a world of increasing individualism, overflow of information and post-factual era, knowing who to rely on and creating rules to assess reliability will be a clear advantage.

SIGNALS AND TRENDS

Trust has a deep impact on the organization's value, both for its shareholders and its stakeholders. "Trust is the conduit of influence; it is the medium through which ideas travel".[196] In fact, the level of trust in business relationships, whether internal with employees or colleagues, or external with clients and partners, is the greatest determinant of success.[197]

Studies have shown that employees who feel trusted are more likely to feel like a useful and important part of an organization and are more likely to stay engaged.[198] Employee trust was shown to be positively related to employee commitment. Both employee engagement and commitment are very strong markers of a sustained productivity.

Conversely, besides reducing workforce productivity, and dramatically increasing turnover, lack of trust will hamper the recruitment of talent, and reduced feedback culture and communication will conceal potential problems.

Yet, in a VUCA world, it is not enough to say that employees always trust leaders when they are consistent between their words and actions, and openly communicate opinions, ideas and information. Undoubtedly, structured work processes with weekly bilateral meetings, quarterly gatherings or regular phone meetings help prevent gaps in communication, increasing trust between employee and manager. "But trust takes on a different meaning in the digital age as many organizations are relying more heavily on virtual teams".[199]

Trust is so paramount that it will eventually be among the characteristics being scrutinized by analysts for ratings, earning calls, and dividends. Organizations will have to build a business case for developing trust,[200] as reduced employee trust level will be quantified in share value.

Trust Portfolio Management is an art. A leader has to excel in it. Trust has manifold components adding to its value (such as credibility, reliability and intimacy) and abhors self-orientation."[201] Data is the new oil – trust is the new gold".

RESPONSIBILITY

Run "trust surveys". Develop a business case for increasing trust. See trust as an equation that leaders can optimize, assess the "trust" level of leaders by breaking it down to its constituent variables and design individual upskilling pathways to reach the ideal Trust Portfolio.

196 Cuddy, A. (2017, March 27). *Trust is the conduit of influence: It is the medium through which ideas travel*. Retrieved from https://twitter.com/amyjccuddy/status/846352108018393088.

197 Understanding the trust equation. Retrieved from https://trustedadvisor.com/why-trust-matters/understanding-trust/understanding-the-trust-equation.

198 Woodruffe, C. (2006). The crucial importance of employee engagement. *Human Resource Management International Digest*.

199 Bosch-Sijtsema & Sivunen, (2013); Crowley, (2016); Ferenc, (2015); Kock, (2000).

200 Sullivan. J. (2018). HR, We have a problem: Up to 80% of employees don't trust us. *Talent Management & HR*.

201 Having a conceptual framework and analytical way of evaluating and understanding trust – such as "The Trust Equation" introduced in 2000 by Harvard professor David Maister – allows for targeted improvement of the overall organization's trustworthiness. Maister, D. H., Green, D. H. & Galford, R. M. (2000). *The trusted advisor*. New York, NY: Free Press.

10. Art of Rewarding

PURPOSE
Rethink remuneration to match a new reality and shifting needs of employees. Adaptative packages, benefits and payments should support aspirations and life trajectories.

EVOLVES FROM
Compensation & benefits
HR law & unions

TRAITS OF FUTURES
1. More, Faster
3. Community
6. Dematerialzed Work
9. Enabling Laws
10. New Value Schemes

MYTHOLOGY

Demigod   Monk

AT A GLANCE   Impact: 7/10
                       Costs: 7/10

Gain a competitive edge

Impact >>

Costs >>

REAL SCALE

Real awareness

Enabling ecosystem

Available technologies

Laid-out action

Total: 3/10

Quote by:
ALAIN SALAMIN
UNIL | HEC Lausanne
Lecturer

Future successful compensation programs will need to better balance external competitivity and internal equity, including gender. They will also become much more flexible, better adapted to individual characteristics, and foster teamwork.

SIGNALS AND TRENDS

Values are shifting and increasingly criticizing our current economic paradigm. Even the Financial Times calls for a reset of capitalism[202]; we see the rise of the Experience Economy and the NOwnership[203] concept. Compensation and benefits as broadly proposed in our economy should be rethought in the light of new needs and interests across generations, to propose the right custom-tailored package to employees.

Fringe benefits, representing only 4.4% in 2017,[204] are mainly offered in the form of a parking space or mobile phone. Offering individualized compensation could represent a competitive advantage in attracting and retaining employees. Lifestyle incentives will be more prevalent,[205] meaning HR will need a deeper understanding of employees' lives and needs. Moreover, the three-stage life (study–work–retire) we are used to is also coming to an end, and new two-dimensional and parallel life trajectories will put value on different elements as life goes on.[206]

Until today, many organizations – in particular the public administrations – have made it a point of honor to develop fair and transparent remuneration systems. This particularity makes the system very inflexible and less and less adapted to a changing reality. Rethinking remuneration with an artistic and creative touch will represent a great competitive advantage when recruiting talents.

Going one step further, in the age of *More, Faster* and *Digital Cleaving's Power*, we could easily imagine the rise of real-time remuneration based on blockchain, maybe starting with the Gig economy but ultimately being deployed in all organizations.

RESPONSIBILITY

Know and understand employees' needs, interests, and values, and dynamically map and exploit them in order to offer a personalized and evolutive tailored compensation package. Create a variable-geometry remuneration system which ensures equal pay among genders within the organization and coherence with the market positioning.

202 FT sets the agenda with new brand platform. (2019). *Financial Times*.
203 Morgan, B. (2019). NOwnership, no problem: An updated look at why Millennials value experiences over owning things. *Forbes*.
204 Plandade, J. (2017). Vers des salaires "à la carte" en Suisse ?. *Bilan*.
205 Donker, Ch. (2017). The way we work – in 2025 and beyond. *PricewaterhouseCoopers*.
206 Gratton, L. & Scott, A. (2016). *The 100-year life living and working in an age of longevity*. London: Bloomsbury.

11. Employee Branding & Avatars

PURPOSE
Transform your employees into "employer's brand" ambassadors for a broader and more effective visibility and impact – in physical reality and in extended realities.

EVOLVES FROM
HR marketing

TRAITS OF FUTURES
1. More, Faster
2. Digital's Cleaving Power
3. Community
6. Dematerialzed Work
10. New Value Schemes

MYTHOLOGY

Demigod   Centaur

AT A GLANCE   Impact: 7/10
                       Costs: 8/10

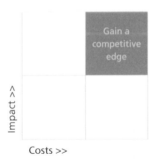

Gain a competitive edge

Impact >>

Costs >>

REAL SCALE

Real awareness

Enabling ecosystem

Available technologies

Laid-out action

Total: 6/10

Quote by:
TARA YIP
Swissquote Bank
Head of Human Resources

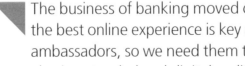 The business of banking moved online years ago. Offering clients the best online experience is key and employees are our best ambassadors, so we need them to proudly represent their institution also in extended and digital realities.

SIGNALS AND TRENDS

If social media shifted marketing power from the brand to the customer, the brand power has also shifted from employers to employees. In a 2018 Randstad survey, 86% of the individuals[207] would not apply or keep working for a company that has a bad reputation with former employees or the general public.[208]

If organizations have worked hard at developing their employer branding strategies, a keystone to attract and retain the right talents, they now must exploit their best source of impact: their employees.

In a world where people trust peers over institutions, in which the borders between private and professional life are blurred, and where individuals "slash" between multiple jobs, Employee Branding aims at influencing and shaping the behavior of an organization's employees so that they project the brand identity in their daily activities – wherever they spend most of their time, be it at work, on social media or sooner in XR.

Since most organizations will all have their digital infrastructure to allow for extensive VR placement, business will happen increasingly in virtual conference centers and virtual convention buildings. To best exploit these realities, HR will manage the branded digital infrastructure and the reputation factor coming with VR presence in business events. Virtual existence in these dematerialized worlds will be rendered possible through the presence of employees under cover of Avatars. Moving beyond employer's and then employees' branding, HR will launch Avatars branding in the Human Cloud[209] and provide employees with branded uniforms or accessories both in the virtual and physical worlds. However unlikely and far-fetched this may seem, it is not. In 2019, a one-of-its-kind digital piece of clothing from a Dutch digital fashion house sold for $9,500.[210]

It has become even easier to imagine purchasing a virtual outfit to wear to a Zoom party now that the COVID-19 crisis has virtualized many reunions and from there to imagining virtual avatar branding is just a step away.

Presenting the organization's colors and visual identity equally in the physical and in the digital slashers' world will increase employer's brand consistency and trust.

RESPONSIBILITY

Support and coach employees on designing and managing their public presence on social networks and in XR, so that they can present the organization's brand in the best possible light. This can mean helping them optimize their LinkedIn profiles – by proposing to standardize and unify images and giving them a corporate visual identity twist – or, in a near future, offer to create effective and branded Avatars to employees to exploit their existence in XR.

207 Which a 2018 Randstad survey clearly confirms. *Your best employees are leaving: But is it personal or practical?* Retrieved from https://rlc.randsta-dusa.com/press-room/press-releases/your-best-employees-are-leaving-but-is-it-personal-or-practical.
208 *Ibid.*
209 Staffing Industry Analysts. (2017). The Human Cloud is an emerging set of work intermediation models that enable work arrangements of various kinds to be established and completed (including payment of workers) entirely through a digital/online platform. In *The Human Cloud, the Gig economy & the transformation of work.* Crain Communications.
210 Marchese, K. (2019). Designers are now selling 'digital clothes' that don't actually exist. *designboom.*

12. Organization Influencer Management

PURPOSE
Look beyond the organization chart and identify internal nodes and influencers to partner with as ambassadors of internal change projects and external employer's brand promoters.

EVOLVES FROM
HR management & operations
HR marketing

TRAITS OF FUTURES
2. Digital's Cleaving Power
4. Trust
6. Dematerialzed Work
10. New Value Schemes

MYTHOLOGY

Centaur   Knight   Monk

AT A GLANCE   Impact: 6/10
                        Costs: 2/10

Act now

Impact >>

Costs >>

REAL SCALE

Real awareness

Enabling ecosystem

Available technologies

Laid-out action

Total: 5/10

Quote by:
GUY ZEHNDER
Firmenich
Director of HR World Operations

Brands are no longer trusted, individuals are. Your best "brand ambassadors" are those delivering impact through authenticity – not just senior leadership. We need a new lens not to miss the influencers in the niches of the organization.

SIGNALS AND TRENDS

Skills obsolescence, Gig economy, rising war for talents, and aging of the population are all elements that have driven the HR function to adopt marketing-like strategies to attract and retain talents.

Marketing has evolved several times over the past decades. It started from paper advertising and TV commercials and moved across time towards management and exploitation of an armada of online media to reach its ever-evolving target: the consumer. Employees happen to also be consumers, and reaching out to them will take the same tools, execution of the same strategies and conquering of the same spaces. A non-exhaustive list, depending on the age of the employee, might encompass Facebook, Twitter, WhatsApp, LinkedIn, Instagram, YouTube, Snapchat, TikTok, not to mention all the social media platforms that will emerge in the near future.

The effectiveness of the influencing messages is derived from the authenticity and the perceived authority of its creator, the influencer – in our case a member of the organization.[211]

The most influential employee rarely is the one we imagine. It takes a thorough analysis of the organizational human network and the collaboration pattern rooted in organization to spot the right individual. This can be done through the power of network analysis, for which many tools already exist.[212]

Nodes, or very influential employees, can be strong internal ambassadors of change and very valuable partners for leaders in the chaotic years to come. They can also be powerful external ambassadors for the employer's brand if their online presence is professionally managed and if they are coached for corporate appearance, authentic behavior as well as for credible communication skills.

Going from hierarchical to scattered organization, from linear to bidimensional career, the interplay of chance, uncertainty, friction, and increased speed of change will have the potential to uncover a rising lack of trust in a higher management and executive level not being up-to-date with the world. Employees will leverage the informal dimension of networking to find someone to relate to and turn to for advice and guidance.

RESPONSIBILITY

Run organizational network analysis (ONA) to identify influencers. Facilitate and support their continuous presence on and in digital platforms and worlds (including internal networks). Develop compelling narratives for them to showcase and valorize the values and culture of the organization.

211 Martineau, P. (2019, 12 June). The WIRED guide to influencers: everything you need to know about engagement, power likes, sponcon, and trust. WIRED.
212 Polinode.com, how-4.com, or starlinks.co to name a few.

With the COVID-19 crisis, future concepts of work have come to the fore. They must be implemented.

Martial Pasquier
University of Lausanne, *Vice-Rector Human Resources & Finance*

13. HAT Capital Management

PURPOSE

While business has been all about "people, people, people" for the last decades, by 2030 it will be all about "people and machines", as augmented humans or humanized machines join the workforce to achieve business success. HR as a function should position itself as the workforce capital master, be it physical, virtual, nomadic, blended, or hybrid, never forgetting our engagements towards the human part of our workforce.

EVOLVES FROM —

TRAITS OF FUTURES

1. More, Faster
2. Digital's Cleaving Power
6. Dematerialzed Work
7. AI & Humans

MYTHOLOGY

Demigod   Centaur   Knight

AT A GLANCE

Impact: 9/10
Costs: 4/10

Impact >>

Costs >>

REAL SCALE

Real awareness

Enabling ecosystem

Available technologies

Laid-out action

Total: 2/10

Quote by:
CHARLOTTE MAZEL-CABASSE
UNIL-EPFL
Digital Humanities Center
Executive Director

 We've always had tools, yet more complex systems are urging us to re-imagine the kind of sociotechnical assemblage we want to form to leverage the economic potential of machines and mitigate the risk of growing inequalities within the workforce.

SIGNALS AND TRENDS

Human-Autonomy Teaming (HAT) emerges in this context from the confluence of two different factors.

Carl B. Frey and Michael Osborns from Oxford opened up an international discussion about the vulnerability of certain job categories at risk of automatization when they told the world in 2013 that 47% of all jobs were susceptible to automation.[213] Since then, the trend has never been stronger, and automation and automatic processes are routinely replacing low skilled tasks in a form of robot or complex AI systems.[214] The COVID-19 crisis exacerbated this trend.

With the accelerating rise of machine capabilities and considering that today's human workforce could theoretically be replaced by machines at 64%,[215] we understand that workforce structures will need to be thoroughly re-engineered.

In parallel, this acceleration of technologies will see new jobs and opportunities emerging up and down the value chain, requiring new skill sets as humans and machines start to team-up and form innovative sociotechnical assemblages.

From factory workers and maintenance experts to operations managers and engineers in robotics, artificial intelligence and automation will reconceive and reshape the concept of work as we know it, in industrial environments as well as in the dematerialized services environment.

Negotiating this turn towards a more integrated human and machine collaboration is a fantastic challenge for organizations that will need to foster a culture of complementarity and reliability instead of competition and rampant inequality. As collaboration and teaming evolves and intensifies, thus creating completely new jobs in self-aware organizations, HR leaders will have to manage a new type of capital – the Human Autonomy Teaming Capital. This is where the skills of autonomous and intelligent systems together with humans, be it in a functional or essential fusion, can no longer be separated and will need to have their own taxonomies and descriptions.

RESPONSIBILITY

Study, improve and integrate the inextricable added value of humans and robots working together in the value network of organizations. Reimagine how we work. Anticipate opportunities and risks of the "Centaur-ization" of humans, and exploit or mitigate them in managing the workforce evolution through continuing education and preparing for fusion skills.[216]

213 Frey, C. B. & Osborne, M. A. (2017, January). The future of employment: How susceptible are jobs to computerisation? *Technological Forecasting and Social Change*. pp. 254–280. Elsevier Inc.

214 Bloom, D. & Prettner, K. (2020). The macroeconomic effects of automation and the role of COVID-19 in reinforcing their dynamics. *VOX EU*.

215 Lalive, R. & Floreano, D. *Ibid*.

216 Daugherty, P. R. & Wilson, H. J. (2018). *Human + machine: Reimagining work in the age of AI*. Harvard Business Press.

14. Skills Curation & Brokering

PURPOSE
Map, understand, structure, and curate the space of skills to allow for an efficient new way of building the organization's skills capital, augmenting its power to execute, and amplifying its evolution to maintain the competitive edge.

EVOLVES FROM
HR recruiting & planning
HR analytics
Learning & development, evaluations

TRAITS OF FUTURES
2. Digital's Cleaving Power
3. Community
7. AI & Humans

MYTHOLOGY

Centaur   Minotaur

AT A GLANCE   Impact: 10/10
                          Costs: 9/10

Gain a competitive edge

Impact >>

Costs >>

REAL SCALE

Real awareness

Enabling ecosystem

Available technologies

Laid-out action

Total: 3/10

Quote by:
RAFAEL LALIVE
UNIL | HEC Lausanne
Professor & Vice-Dean

 People have such rich and amazing skill portfolios.
Skills curation and brokering helps them unleash their full potential.

SIGNALS AND TRENDS

Skills gap, shortage, mismatch, or obsolescence are no buzzwords; they represent a real risk in the current economy, and therefore are non-negligible national security threats. The skills issue has been aggravated by the COVID-19 crisis, which accelerated the digitalization of work and thus the need for more digital skills across the workforce. Digital skills are by no means the only skills that will be needed in the future. New types of skills, such as soft, cognitive, fusion or amplifying skills, are already in demand and will increasingly be over the next ten years.

The *Digital's Cleaving Power* has allowed for coupling, decoupling and re-coupling of features of the world. Location and presence are not coupled anymore and neither do law and territory, or usage and ownership.[217] Digitalization had the same effect on work, unbundling it into tasks and then into skills, allowing for more granular understanding, control, de-construction and re-bundling[218]; a job is not tied to just one individual anymore – skills are.

Surfing on the growing need for skills management and enabled by technology, emerging AI-driven tools for skills matching and anticipation do not address the matching of people and jobs anymore. When looking at skills, we see that individuals could easily and successfully move away from their job families to totally new jobs in two-thirds of the cases.[219]

In parallel, globalization and dematerialization of services have allowed for a rise of the Gig economy and telemigration.[220] Digital platforms enhance skills demand and offer to meet at the equilibrium price in the virtual marketplace, irrespective of location or territoriality.

Moreover, by 2030 5G and 6G will virtually allow for increased remote work, even with very complex jobs requiring highly specialized skills, thus allowing for reverse brain-drain and shifting the global geo-labor equilibrium.

For the organization, performing a job is thus no longer tied to one "performer" or even to a place; in the future, the very notion of "employee" could well be composed as a mosaic of skills sourced from all over the planet. Diplomas are no longer a skills guarantee, and skills curators will need to "separate the wheat from the chaff".

RESPONSIBILITY

Perform "work-task planning", [221] identify the best source of skills, irrespectively of location and territoriality, and manage to buy, borrow, or build the ideal skillset for the organization to perform.

Move away from job descriptions and skip the description of job families, shifting towards a map of skills gaps and needs.

217 Floridi, L. (2017). Digital's cleaving power and its consequences. *Philosophy & Technology*, 30, 123–129.

218 Bolles, G.A. (2017). Unbundling work: Learning to thrive in disruptive times. Retrieved from https://medium.com/@gbolles/unbundling-work-learning-to-thrive-in-disruptive-times-427b172b1470.

219 Lalive, R. & Floreano, D. (2021 in press). *Fighting human obsolescence in a world disrupted by machines*. HEC Lausanne UNIL – EPFL.

220 Baldwin, R. (2019). *The globotics upheaval: Globalization, robotics, and the future of work*. UK: Oxford University Press.

221 Ulrich, D. (2020). Four innovations that will transform talent management forever. *TalentQ*.

15. Human Predictive Maintenance

PURPOSE
Turn the tables on AI. As much as AI can be considered the very source of the rampant skills obsolescence, AI-enabled human predictive maintenance could and should be the solution to upskill or reskill towards the right skills set and to foster a lifelong learning culture.

EVOLVES FROM
Learning & development, evaluations

TRAITS OF FUTURES
1. More, Faster
5. Centaurs & Knights
7. AI & Humans
9. Enabling Laws

MYTHOLOGY

Knight   Minotaur

AT A GLANCE
Impact: 8/10
Costs: 10/10

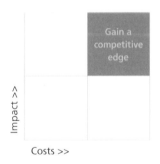

Gain a competitive edge

Impact >>

Costs >>

REAL SCALE

Real awareness

Enabling ecosystem

Available technologies

Laid-out action

Total: 4/10

Quote by:
DANIEL SAMAAN
International Labour Organization
Senior Economist

 We will have to embrace the new capabilities of AI to make sense of HR data. Human resource management in 2030 will include data scientists and strategic thinkers who advise the CEO about the organization's skills portfolio and how to steer it.

SIGNALS AND TRENDS

If Human Skills Obsolescence represents a national security threat, it also represents a threat to businesses, where jobs have become digitalized and automated, and where humans are increasingly "augmented" and have naturally integrated machines into their daily lives. Machines and humans are increasingly connected. Greater human-machine collaboration is inevitable and necessary. In the short term, the Future of Work is "job-sharing" with machines, whereas humans – in order to remain relevant – must identify and constantly offer new added value to their organizations.

In the same way as industry performs "machine predictive maintenance" to compute the Remaining Useful Life (RUL) of machines and to target maintenance to extend the life of a product, the HR function will be led to run "Human predictive maintenance" with the objective to compute the Remaining Relevant Life (RRL) of employees. It will also find ways to extend the period of prevalence of individuals in the organization by developing and offering targeted re-skilling or upskilling.

As already stated by McKinsey in 2017,[222] the challenge for the coming decades will be to create effective large-scale career transition programs. The urgency of work will invariably trump the luxury of learning. Considering that 80% of CEOs now believe the need for new skills is their biggest business challenge,[223] we will need new ways of making lifelong learning work. "Learning in the flow of work" is a way to realize the objective of learning while inflecting it with the boundary conditions of the world of work: for learning to really happen, it must be aligned and fit into working days and lives,

proposing tailor made content.[224] Cutting-edge technology today allows the curating and pushing of content that is relevant, rich, and timely, to build solutions and experiences that make learning almost invisible in our jobs.

Yet part of the challenge is that executives in most cases are still lagging behind when it comes to identifying the skills necessary to succeed in an ever-changing world of "4.0". Understanding the skills that will be needed tomorrow is a high priority for the 60% that are heavily investing in trying to understand where to develop their staff [225] to maintain their pertinence within the workforce.

By 2030, services using natural language processing will be able to capture an employee's skills DNA in real-time and assess it against the needs of the organization and immediately infer skills gap and reskilling needs.

RESPONSIBILITY

Capture employee's skills and assess them with the organization's current or future needs. Maintain a database of skills and ensure evolution of the used taxonomy. Link continuing education initiatives with the identified skills gaps to avoid employees falling into obsolescence and lack of pertinence.

222 Manyika, J. et al. (2017). Jobs lost – jobs gained. *McKinsey Global Institute*.
223 Moritz, B. E. (2020). PricewaterhouseCoopers 23rd annual global ceo survey – navigating the rising tide of uncertainty. *PricewaterhouseCoopers*.
224 Bersin, J. & Zao-Sanders, M. (2019). Making learning a part of everyday work. *Harvard Business Review*.
225 Renjen, P. (2020). Industry 4.0: At the intersection of readiness and responsibility. *Deloitte Insights*.

16. XR Presence Management

PURPOSE
Ensure that the organization has a strong identity in extended worlds, maintaining a lively and constant presence, as a source of competitive advantage in brand value, positioning, and talent attraction.

EVOLVES FROM
HR marketing

TRAITS OF FUTURES
4. Trust
6. Dematerialzed Work
8. Opportunities
10. New Value Schemes

MYTHOLOGY

Knight   Minotaur

AT A GLANCE   Impact: 5/10
                        Costs: 9/10

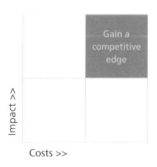

Gain a competitive edge

Impact >>

Costs >>

REAL SCALE

Real awareness

Enabling ecosystem

Available technologies

Laid-out action

Total: 3/10

Quote by:
JULIEN HAUTLE
Swisscom (Suisse) SA
Future Workforce Manager

 With organizational borders continuing to fade away, the importance of a trustworthy and motivating employer value proposition increases. People want to be proud of social constructs they are a part of – HR needs to cultivate those values.

SIGNALS AND TRENDS

The digital conference platform ZOOM was downloaded 2.13m times around the world on 23 March 2020, the day the lockdown was announced in the UK – up from 56,000 a day two months earlier.[226] While the COVID-19 pandemic represented an unprecedented acceleration of digitalization of the world of work, the trend had been there since long ago. Past the crisis, there is a fair chance that working habits will experience a level of hysteresis by this strain, never coming back to the old normal and maintaining a certain form of distance, when not being totally "remotized".

The rise of immersive video games, where individuals live their second lives, is no longer a weak signal but a clear trend.

In 2030, technology will have exponentially evolved, and virtual reality will no longer be considered "not real", having achieved photorealism and real-time environment streaming. It will have the ability to alter our perception of reality, or better, extend it. By 2030 the adoption of VR, AR, and XR will be broad in the fields of healthcare or engineering operations. There might also be virtual organizations standing in a world that does not exist per se, and workers will meet, socialize, and collaborate immersed in virtual *loci*, not existing in physical dimensions. The very concept of "existence" might be challenged in its original meaning.

Just as companies are investing intensely for product placements in virtual worlds, especially in video games, organizations will market their values, purposes and benefits as employers in emerging extended worlds, to reach out to the best talents regardless of their physical location. An obvious collateral effect will be the redistribution of priorities for workplace investments. Boasting large corporate offices downtown with gravity-challenging architectures will no longer be a competitive advantage to position the organization and recruit talents. We will see a shift and it will be slowly equally important to have a bespoke, state-of-the-art digital infrastructure and corporate and delivery processes that will empower remotely working employees.

RESPONSIBILITY

Arrange for solid links between physical and extended reality to preserve their primacy, while integrating and valorizing the local culture and company values within the extended reality space.

226 Neate, R. (2020, 31 March). Zoom booms as demand for video-conferencing tech grows. *The Guardian*.

17. Transgenerational Bridging

PURPOSE
Exploit the breadth and depth of "memory" of seniors, and the high level of "processing power" of juniors, so that organizations can get the best of both generations, safeguarding their stability and guaranteeing their resilience – at once.

EVOLVES FROM   —

TRAITS OF FUTURES
2. Digital's Cleaving Power
4. Trust
5. Centaurs & Knights
8. Opportunities
10. New Value Schemes

MYTHOLOGY

Demigod   Knight

AT A GLANCE   Impact: 6/10
                     Costs: 4/10

Act now

Impact >>

Costs >>

REAL SCALE

Real awareness

Enabling ecosystem

Available technologies

Laid-out action

Total: 7/10

Quote by:
KARINE LAMMLE
Tetra Pak
Head of HR Country Services Switzerland

 Numerous great employees will soon go on retirement. Younger generations will enter the labor force with new abilities and expectations. It is imperative that we build bridges between generations to exploit the best of both worlds.

SIGNALS AND TRENDS

Senior management and highly experienced individuals within the organization are the treasure of its "institutional intelligence". Coping with the loss of institutional intelligence as the Baby Boomer generation retires will be one of the major challenges of the next decade. Some companies may see up to 50% of their workforce leave the labor market within the next 10 years.[227] The Swiss Employers' Association issued a warning in early 2020 on Switzerland facing a shortage of 700,000 workers in ten years' time, due mainly to retirement of the Baby Boomer generation.[228] Even if Switzerland remains attractive for skilled workers and if immigration could be a key to plug the gap, this inverted age pyramid is going to impact organizations, starting with those enjoying a high level of loyalty and senior employees. Seeing senior employees leave will mean the loss of an immense well of knowledge, which younger generations will not be able to replace.[229]

Born in the age of infinite data and immediate access to information, newer generations have their brains wired differently, allowing for the development of new abilities but missing out on some cognitive traits of the former generation.[230] Not only are we facing a growing risk of employee shortage due to demographic shifts, but we are at risk of seeing heritage skillsets disappear from the labor market altogether.

Moreover, growing in a world of non-linear career paths, juniors face work with a different attitude. Whereas seniors represent stability, loyalty and thus *security*, juniors bring along instability, agility and thus *resilience* – all of which being highly necessary in troubled times.

RESPONSIBILITY

Plan dynamic and adaptive employment schemes to keep seniors integrated in the active workforce of the organization for as long as they can and want. Organize and influence social and professional exchanges to foster intergenerational know-how and value transfer (such as mentoring and reverse mentoring/shadowing).

227 Authors' discussions with several mid-sized organizations' leaders in Switzerland.
228 Expat Guide to Switzerland | Expatica. (2020). *Switzerland could 'lack 700,000 workers' in decade's time.*
229 *Ibid.*
230 Anderson, J. & Rainie, L. (2012). Millennials will benefit and suffer due to their hyperconnected lives. *Pew Research Center: Internet, Science & Tech.*

18. Strategic Sustainability In-Casting

PURPOSE
"Walk the sustainable talk", support and guide employees to design their own activities – in and outside their work field – to bring an active part towards a more sustainable posture.

EVOLVES FROM
HR strategy
HR marketing

TRAITS OF FUTURES
8. Opportunities
9. Enabling Laws
10. New Value Schemes

MYTHOLOGY

Demigod   Knight   Monk

AT A GLANCE   Impact: 9/10
                       Costs: 4/10

Act now

Impact >>

Costs >>

REAL SCALE

Real awareness

Enabling ecosystem

Available technologies

Laid-out action

Total: 8/10

Quote by:
BARBARA LAX
Little Green House SA
Founding Director

New generations know that their future is at stake and that sustainability is a key variable in their life equation. To attract the best talents, organizations will have to include environmental, ethical and social purpose in their core mission.

SIGNALS AND TRENDS

More than philanthropy, investing in strategic sustainability to reach the SDGs represents a $12 trillion opportunity for the private sector.[231] This argument alone should propel sustainability to the top of an organization's objectives. Given the growing value placed on a company's CSR practices by Millennials and the impending explosion of Millennials in the workplace, sustainability must become part of the company's recruitment strategy to attract top talent. Sustainability is not only crucial to recruiting talented employees, it is now more than ever a great way to maintain the engagement of your existing workforce.[232]

Generation Z will soon enter the workforce and their expectations are clear – among them, the respect for our planet. Labels such as B Corp[233] are gaining traction in the current marketplace for old and new players to compete in this novel arena, on the one hand for visibility, and on the other hand to fulfill their responsibility at large towards the society.

Human Resources as a function will have to bear the burden and the honor of moving the employees towards a higher awareness of what sustainability is and how it can be acted upon. For instance, considering that a major portion of global warming is caused by anthropogenic activities, calculating Carbon Footprint (CFP) is a natural first step towards making quantifiable actions for emissions reduction. Quite a number of organizations have estimated their CFP nowadays, but besides analyzing their workforce's commute and their environmental impact, little have gone to a more granular level to analyze the global employees' CFP. Since employees' motivation and commitment will be affected by the extent to which they can align their personal identity and image with that of the organization, organizations should allow employees to codesign sustainable practices by seeking their input and crowdsourcing internal ideas to enhance the organization's sustainability efforts.

RESPONSIBILITY

Integrate concepts such as circular economy or SDGs in the organization's language and create a sustainability common ground, language and culture through experiments and new processes. Crowdsource internal ideas to improve the organization's processes and the employees' overall environmental impact. Design CFP computing models for employees and propose applicable solutions to employees to minimize their impact on the environment. Give employees the opportunity to offer their time to a noble environmental or societal cause during their working hours.

231 Vali, N. (2017). More than philanthropy: SDGs are a $12 trillion opportunity for the private sector. *United Nations Development Programme*.
232 Meister, J. (2012). Corporate social responsibility: A lever for employee attraction and engagement. *Forbes*.
233 See https://bcorporation.net/.

Any useful idea about the futures should appear to be ridiculous.

Dator's Second Law of the Future

Jim Dator
Professor Emeritus and former Director of the Hawaii Research Center for Futures Studies

19. A–Z Resilience

PURPOSE
Anticipate and prepare human capital to help organizations thrive, and be ready to recover quickly from difficulties. Ensure rapid and smooth adaptation to unexpected change, both in terms of organizational structure and emotional agility.

EVOLVES FROM
HR strategy
Learning & development, evaluations
HR innovation

TRAITS OF FUTURES
1. More, Faster
4. Trust
7. AI & Humans
10. New Value Schemes

MYTHOLOGY

Demigod   Centaur

AT A GLANCE   Impact: 9/10
                     Costs: 10/10

Gain a competitive edge

Impact >>

Costs >>

REAL SCALE

Real awareness

Enabling ecosystem

Available technologies

Laid-out action

Total: 6/10

Quote by:
BERTRAND LANXADE
Mazars
Head of Human Resources

In the turmoil facing the world of work, inner calmness, foresight and courage will be key to boost individual and ultimately organizational resilience. HR needs to create communities of workers and accelerate learning to develop shared resilience.

SIGNALS AND TRENDS

Resilience is the resource against existential threat. Resilience is the ability of an organization (be it a company or a community, service, area or infrastructure) to detect, prevent, and if necessary, to withstand, handle and recover from disruptive challenges enduring over time, sustaining and reacting to strategic shocks, while maintaining the ability to operate with success.

The Resilience Cycle is articulated over five phases: Prepare, Withstand, Absorb, Recover, and Adapt.[234] In this sense, resilience does not happen after a critical event has occurred: it begins way earlier and includes capabilities that are useful prior to adversity.[235] Amid a pandemic, terms like crisis or disruption are on everyone's lips. However, company-specific or market-specific crises happen far more often than we may think. Unfriendly takeovers, mergers and acquisitions, or changes of CEO can be viewed as crises, calling upon organizational resilience. Considering the potential rise of cyber and global climate events or political instability, organizations cannot stand still, unprepared, and waiting for Black Swans[236] to hit. They must anticipate and structure themselves for resilience.

The role the HR function can play in this picture is paramount. Resilience calls for "distributed control with centralized coordination", implying high-quality, real-time data as well as an attentive and empathic leadership rooted in a community. Moreover, resilience is also about facing a growing global uncertainty, the lack of career projection, the growing war for talents or dealing with multidimensional careers with serenity and faith.[237] To navigate this new necessity, organizations will have to develop a resilience strategy and identify metrics for assessment.

RESPONSIBILITY

Develop anticipatory skills among workers and collect/crowd-source ideas to improve current work processes for a more agile organization. Run regular Black Swan environmental and horizon scanning events with teams to identify and prepare for exogenous or endogenous shocks that could alter the organization's operations. Run a skills diversification strategy and hire diverse employee profiles, decentralize operations, and dematerialize work and processes. Apply circular economy concepts to skills and talents and give people a purpose to believe in. Run resilience workshop to grow employees' internal strength to cope with the stress imposed by a world increasingly volatile, uncertain, complex and ambiguous (VUCA).

234 NATO Collaborative Resilience (CoRe) Capstone Concept Vision. (2019).
235 Duchek, S., Raetze, S. & Ianina Scheuch, I. (2019). The role of diversity in organizational resilience: A theoretical framework. *Business Research*.
236 According to Oxford Languages, a Black Swan is "an unpredictable or unforeseen event, typically one with extreme consequences".
237 Bersin, J. (2020). *Can we make our organizations resilient? And make society resilient as a result?*. Josh Bersin Blog.

20. Health, Hope & Happiness Empowerment

PURPOSE
Map, monitor, manage and take care of physical and emotional states of employees to maintain workforce productivity and stability.

EVOLVES FROM
HR management & operations
HR risks & complaints
HR marketing

TRAITS OF FUTURES
1. More, Faster
4. Trust
10. New Value Schemes

MYTHOLOGY

Demigod

Monk

AT A GLANCE
Impact: 6/10
Costs: 8/10

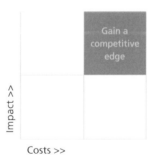

Gain a competitive edge

Impact >>

Costs >>

REAL SCALE

Real awareness

Enabling ecosystem

Available technologies

Laid-out action

Total: 5/10

Quote by:
DAVID VERNEZ
Center for Primary Care
& Public Health (Unisanté)
Head of Department

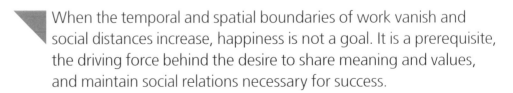
When the temporal and spatial boundaries of work vanish and social distances increase, happiness is not a goal. It is a prerequisite, the driving force behind the desire to share meaning and values, and maintain social relations necessary for success.

SIGNALS AND TRENDS

Numerous studies[238] have highlighted a clear negative correlation between happiness and absenteeism, and a clear positive correlation between satisfaction and performance. The happier the employee, the higher the productivity. Those links provide a strong business case for organization to focus on employee happiness, which is no longer considered as "nice to have" but as an important and potentially imperative employee factor to work.

Psychological well-being is linked with having deep sincere contacts, being a valued member of an enduring social group, and being enmeshed in a network of extended kin. Consequently the current conditions of modern working – increasingly happening in virtual worlds, or involving "cobots"[239] rather than colleagues – do not seem to be setting up to increase human happiness. However, it seems clear that modern humans cannot go back in time and live the lives of their Stone Age ancestors, nor would a move in that direction be inherently desirable, given that technology and industrial revolutions have eliminated many of the hostile forces of nature that formerly made life brutish, painful, and short.[240] Thus, for organizations to remain a place and a source of happiness, they have to assess how happiness drivers are being altered by technological and societal changes and changing value schemes.

In the wake of the COVID-19 crisis, the fear of a more hazardous and less social working life, new organizational structures must emerge, which support and empower employee health, hope and happiness. In the new world of work, it will be paramount to be able to manage not time but positive energy and hope. "Hope doesn't demarcate a linear path, but it does guide us through twists and turns. Hope views the glass as half full, not half empty. Hope supports realistic optimism, a necessary component of success". [241] In order to feel sufficiently energetic and faithful every day, organizations need to shift to investing in employees' health and well-being, rather than focusing on getting the most out of them. Employees should be encouraged to introduce periods of "recreation" and "re-creation" and have the autonomy to do this in a way that works for them.[242] Besides, since the 2020 world pandemic has bestowed a lasting impact on our society and in our organizations forcing social distancing, it will be increasingly necessary to introduce forms of distance socializing.

RESPONSIBILITY

Align company purpose and organizational structure and processes to employees' physical and emotional needs to ensure the individuals' livelihood and to safeguard health via clear and rigorous regulations. Manage onlife risks and deviations and prevent burnouts. Guarantee ergonomic and inspiring offices and propose a state-of-the-art digital environment to allow for greater emotional closeness between colleagues, despite physical distance.

238 Hoxsey, D. (2010). Are Happy employees healthy employees? Researching the effects of employee engagement on absenteeism. *Canadian Public Administration*, 53(4), 551–571.
239 Green, T. (2016). Webcast: Job-safe cobots: liability & safety issues. *Robotics Business Review*.
240 Hoxsey, D. (2010). *Ibid*.
241 Mills-Scofield, D. (2012, 9 October). Hope is a strategy (well, sort of). *Harvard Business Review*.
242 Gratton, L. & Scott, A. (2016). *The 100-year life living and working in an age of longevity*. London, Bloomsbury.

21. Onlife Performance Management

PURPOSE
Evaluate employee's performance
in a world of work where the borders
between private and professional
life are blurred by the constant hypo-
connectivity, in which a company's targets
are moving and where the presence
of a worker need not be identical
to its location.

EVOLVES FROM
Learning & development, evaluations
HR law & unions

TRAITS OF FUTURES
2. Digital's Cleaving Power
4. Trust
6. Dematerialzed Work
9. Enabling Laws
10. New Value Schemes

MYTHOLOGY

Centaur   Knight

AT A GLANCE   Impact: 9/10
                       Costs: 6/10

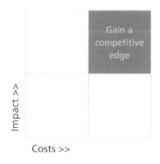

Gain a competitive edge

Impact >>

Costs >>

REAL SCALE

Real awareness

Enabling ecosystem

Available technologies

Laid-out action

Total: 5/10

Quote by:
LAURE HAUSWIRTH
City of Morges
Head of HR Department

The world of work has gone online and the trend seems here
to stay. How can line managers motivate, lead and preserve their
teams, let alone evaluate them? HR will need to develop
and propose new tools and guidelines to managing onlife teams.

SIGNALS AND TRENDS

Employees are the main capital to create value within organizations, thus their performance needs to be scrutinized, evaluated, maintained, or improved to increase the organizations' overall performance.

Performance management, as assessed today, is an "ongoing process of communication between a supervisor and an employee that occurs throughout the year, in support of accomplishing the strategic objectives of the organization. The communication process includes clarifying expectations, setting objectives, identifying goals, providing feedback, and reviewing results".[243] If the organization's target is no longer stable and moves constantly to adapt to the flow, and if the organization's setting and processes evolve accordingly, setting objectives or providing feedback once or twice a year will not suffice.

All the more so, the employees themselves experienced their own values and own self-perception disrupted, and their way of working and socializing transformed by the surrounding hyper connectivity and growing information and communication technology (ICT) prevalence. Indeed, in every aspect of life, ICT has become an environmental force creating and transforming our realities.[244] While former generations think in terms of online/offline, AI natives are always "onlife".[245] It is HR's role to assess the performance of a transgenerational workforce integrating these specificities.

Hyperconnectivity confronts us with both benefits and challenges. It can be a powerful tool for collaboration that drives global alignment and increased efficiency.[246] In parallel, the risk of onlife is escapism (absence), absorption (attention) and alienation (distraction),[247] all of which have a strong impact of performance.

Assessing performance under such conditions becomes tricky and calls for an evolution of the discipline.

RESPONSIBILITY

Move towards general collaborative tools to follow employees' activities and to allow constant interaction and access needed in the onlife way of work. Keep track of employees' online activities to monitor their activity and prevent burnouts or bore-outs. Create boundaries between online activities linked to professional performance and private life online activities. Develop a trust-based self-evaluation methodology to reconcile the invisible (online) and the visible (in life), to compute the "onlife" performance level.

243 Berkeley people & culture. (1991). *Performance management: Concepts & definitions.*

244 Passarelli, B. & Grieco Cabral de Mello Vetritti, F. (2016). #ConnectedYouthBrazil Research: Emerging literacies in a hyperconnected society. *In Handbook of research on comparative approaches to the digital age revolution in Europe and the Americas* (Chapter 11, pp. 171–191). IGI Global.

245 Floridi, L. (Ed.). (2015). *The onlife manifesto: Being human in a hyper-connected era.* Cham: Springer International Publishing.

246 Pastore, M. & People Matters Media Pvt Ltd.(2016). Hyperconnectivity and its impact on workplace. *People Matters.*

247 Floridi, L. (2017). *Happiness onlife.* Keynote to Sogeti Research Institute for the Analysis of New Technology (VINT) event "The Pursuit of Digital Happiness". Retrieved from https://www.slideshare.net/sogeti_nl/luciano-floridi-76925492.

22. HR Hacktivism

PURPOSE
Create high-risk, high-value alternatives for HR to be prepared for the unforeseen and amplify organizational resilience. Be a constant source of ideas and projects for HR Adaptation.

EVOLVES FROM
HR management & operations

TRAITS OF FUTURES
4. Trust
5. Centaurs & Knights
6. Dematerialzed Work
8. Opportunities

MYTHOLOGY

Centaur   Knight

AT A GLANCE   Impact: 4/10
                       Costs: 7/10

Impact >>

Prepare for the unthinkable

Costs >>

REAL SCALE

Real awareness

Enabling ecosystem

Available technologies

Laid-out action

Total: 5/10

Quote by:
YVES EPINEY
Direction Plus SA
Associate Partner

HR should anticipate issues before they arise. They should build an enabling environment and develop a culture of audacity to allow the organization's internal forces to generate original and creative solutions for growing challenges.

SIGNALS AND TRENDS

Hacktivism: derived from the portmanteau of 'Hack' and 'Activism', hacktivism is the act of hacking, or breaking into a computer system, for politically or socially motivated purposes.

Far from being online terrorists or thrill-seekers, hacktivists open themselves to collaborating with other organizations that previously inhabited vastly different worlds, to create a tentative *esprit de corps* to solve growing issues.

To set the right perspective, it is fundamental to remember that constant disruptions call for agility, creativity, and preparedness for the unexpected. "Hacking" HR here means to find the angle not seen, explore the road not taken, challenge the established paradigms, and thrive in unorthodoxy and this in a very rapid and agile process.

The Discipline of HR hacktivism encompasses a passion for tinkering and noodling around new, expansionary or even radical concepts, playing with ambidextrous ideas. It should organize red teaming and reverse brainstorming on everything HR. Examples of ideas to be tackled in this setting could be understanding unspoken forces at work – strengthening a praxis of complacency – and finding possible ways to integrate them into a more successful corporate culture,[248] or even experimenting with new values schemes and how they can empower the organization.[249]

One of HR Hacktivism's duties would be to design and run hackathons. The idea of a hackathon, i.e. creating a hack or project in a succinct amount of time, most often overnight, is not unique to technology or computer science. It is now widely spread in environmental projects and has started to reach the HR community a few years back. Easy to organize, relatively cheap, hackathons are great for having people and ideas collide and spark innovations.

RESPONSIBILITY

Conduct structured or unstructured exploration of possibilities. Draft canvases for presentations of batches of ideas. Experiment within the boundaries of the unit or function.

248 Weil, D. (2014). The *fissured workplace*. Harvard University Press.
249 ILO. (2019). *ILO Centenary Declaration for the Future of Work, 2019*. Retrieved from https://www.ilo.org/global/about-the-ilo/mission-and-objectives/centenary-declaration/lang--en/index.htm.

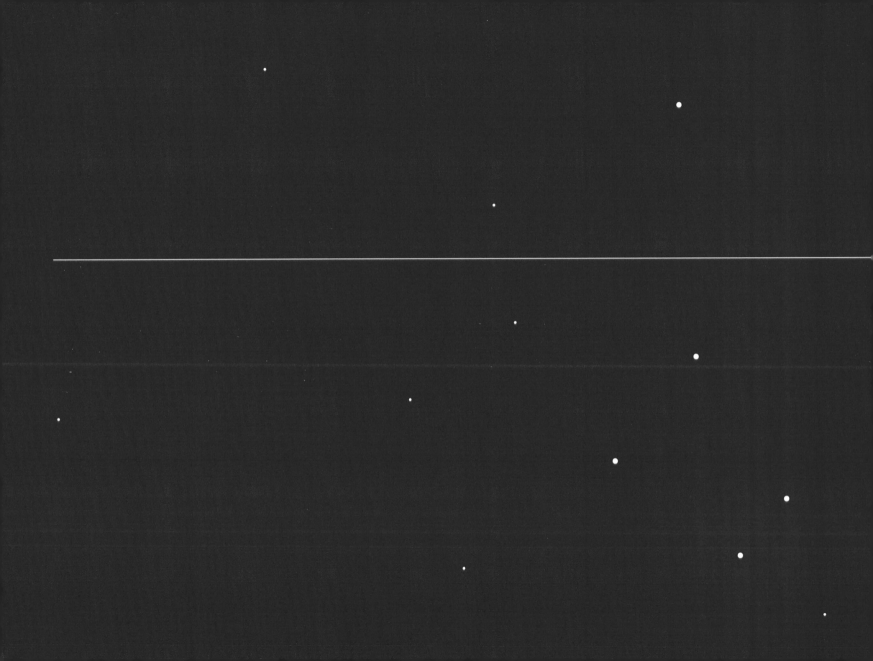

DEVELOPMENT GUIDELINES

FOR INDIVIDUALS

> *Learning, re-skilling, upskilling is going to be a huge issue.*
>
> Satya Nadella, Microsoft CEO

"Lifelong learning is the life-wide voluntary and self-motivated pursuit of knowledge, for not only personal but professional reasons as well. It does not only enhance social inclusion, active citizenship and individual development, but also increases competitiveness and employability".[250] The importance of lifelong learning has been increasingly cited as a key element of the Future of Work. One of the main reasons is increased life expectancy, allowing for many different careers in one single life. Another one is the acceleration of changes, due to convergence of innovation and technologies, which shortens the relevance of certain professions, thus making regular professional reorientation necessary.

Trends like self-management and self-isolation on social media reflect a broad societal move away from collective commitment and towards a more individual focus. Against this backdrop, who is responsible for lifelong learning[251] – the individual, the employer or the state?

It is increasingly important for everyone to self-motivate and make relevant training choices, in line with the current and future labor market's needs, as well as with their own preferences.

A 2020 Deloitte global Human Capital Trends survey[252] shows that while a little over half of the survey respondents consider individuals responsible for their own upskilling, 73% of them reckon that employers ought to take responsibility for developing training opportunities.

We believe that continuing education should be a shared effort including educational institutions, governments, unions, employers and individuals. In this still uncoordinated effort, it is increasingly important for everyone to self-motivate and make relevant training choices, in line with the current and future labor market's needs, as well as with their own preferences. There is a growing number of startups offering data-driven and skills-driven professional reorientation guidelines to ease upskilling actions and transitions.[253] Besides, there are various psychometric tests based on advanced psychological research, offering very insightful guidance for individuals in their quest for ideal reorientation.

With the following guidelines, we would like to offer individuals a different and complementary reading of their own situations, allowing them to orient their curiosity and actions along their Mythology.

250 Ates, H. & Alsal, K. (2012). The importance of lifelong learning has been increasing. Procedia – Social and Behavioral Sciences, 46.
251 Castle, D. (2019). Lifelong learning: An individual or collective concern? Digitalswitzerland.
252 Vuilini, E. (2020). Beyond reskilling: Investing in resilience for uncertain futures. Deloitte Insights.
253 Such as: Faethm.ai, Eightfold.ai, or Jobkred.com to name a few.

Demigods

④ HR Transformation
⑨ Trust Portfolio Management
⑩ Art of Rewarding
⑪ Employee Branding & Avatars
⑬ HAT Capital Management
⑰ Transgenerational Bridging
⑱ Strategic Sustainability In-Casting
⑲ A–Z Resilience
⑳ Health, Hope & Happiness Empowerment
㉒ HR Hacktivism

Centaurs

② Aspirations & Life Design
③ Know Your Employee (KYE)
④ HR Transformation
⑦ Diversity Advantaging
⑧ HR Predictive Analytics
⑨ Trust Portfolio Management
⑪ Employee Branding & Avatars
⑫ Organization Influencer Management
⑬ HAT Capital Management
⑭ Skills Curation & Brokering
⑲ A–Z Resilience
㉑ Onlife Performance Management
㉒ HR Hacktivism

Knights

1 Dynamic Workforce Engagement
2 Aspirations & Life Design
3 Know Your Employee (KYE)
5 HR Adaptation
6 HR Process Re-Engineering
7 Diversity Advantaging
12 Organization Influencer Management
13 HAT Capital Management
15 Human Predictive Maintenance
16 XR Presence Management
17 Transgenerational Bridging
18 Strategic Sustainability In-Casting
21 Onlife Performance Management
22 HR Hacktivism

Minotaurs

5 HR Adaptation
6 HR Process Re-Engineering
8 HR Predictive Analytics
14 Skills Curation & Brokering
15 Human Predictive Maintenance
16 XR Presence Management

Monks

FOR ORGANIZATIONS

*Do what you do best
and outsource the rest.*

Peter Drucker, Professor of Management, 1909–2005

Constellations

Just as with facing the COVID-19 crisis, depending on the size and type of their organizations, HR leaders are not all armed in the same way to deal with unexpected situations the new world of work is bringing along.

The avalanche of change that is waiting just out of our doorstep, like the rise of the Gig economy, the datafication of employees, or the impact of new societal value schemes are changing the landscape in which organizations and especially HR operate. Just as with facing the COVID-19 crisis, depending on the size and type of their organizations, HR leaders are not all armed in the same way to deal with unexpected situations the new world of work is bringing along.

Whereas SMEs can hardly implement cost-intensive HR systems, Public Administrations (PAs) and Multinationals (Multis) are more likely to launch long-term initiatives with little short-term return on investment. While PAs are more limited in their HR innovation scope, since they have stricter reporting and legal constraints, SMEs and Multis enjoy much more freedom.

The following chapter introduces HR specificities of SMEs, PAs and Multis to help define three different and tailored HR development strategies. Indeed, depending on the size and the type of the organization and subsequently the most likely level of complexity of its HR department, the skills available and required in the business, the specific legal or organizational constraints imposed on an industry and on specific companies, will greatly differ.

Regardless of their size, several employers manage HR operations themselves. However, the rise of the complexity linked with internal HR handling in times of disruptions is extremely time-consuming, and distracts leadership from managing core business matters. Smaller companies will find it increasingly difficult to direct growth issues or fast-evolving novelties eroding their core business and at the same time integrating the latest HR developments. To minimize the growing challenges linked with HR management, organizations can outsource almost all or part of their HR activities. Today HR outsourcing companies offer HR services that support organizations throughout the entire employee lifecycle, and typically can take care of services such as payroll, employee benefits, recruiting, etc. With new HR disciplines arising, we will see current HR outsourcing service companies and new startups tackling those new challenges and offering brand new outsourced HR services.

For sure, the option of the qualified hire from these highly skilled and exclusive gardens to grow a full-fledged future-proof HR is always available, but due to time or cost constraints might not be feasible for all organizations, neither meaningful for smaller companies. Outsourcing HR could show two immediate perks: first, providing more time to address issues outside HR; and second, especially for smaller employers, staying up-to-date with the new rules and regulations, and reducing compliance risks. HR outsourcing could mean having an external compass aligning HR operations with business strategy, thus setting a course for future growth.[254]

Consequently, the selection criteria chosen to define the scope and size of each of the following constellations is the estimated level of potential outsourceability of each new discipline and their REAL scale level presented earlier in the book; both these criteria appeared to be pertinent and relevant to propose an insightful choice among the new HR disciplines to be implemented as a priority depending on the status of the organization.

The rise of the complexity linked with internal HR handling in times of disruptions is extremely time-consuming, and distracts leadership from managing core business matters.

254 Dembrowski, P. (n.d.) Benefits of HR outsourcing – why it may be a smart decision. *Connecticut Innovations*.

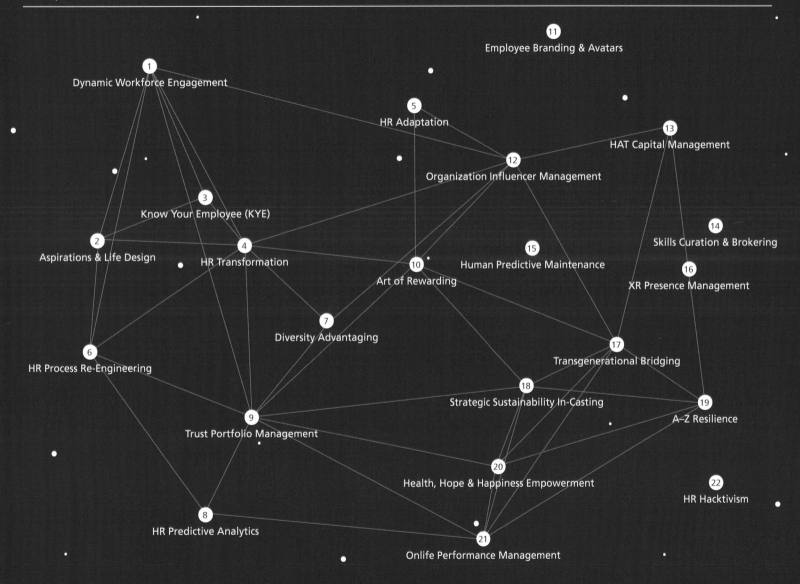

1 Dynamic Workforce Engagement

11 Employee Branding & Avatars

5 HR Adaptation

13 HAT Capital Management

12 Organization Influencer Management

3 Know Your Employee (KYE)

14 Skills Curation & Brokering

2 Aspirations & Life Design

4 HR Transformation

15 Human Predictive Maintenance

16 XR Presence Management

10 Art of Rewarding

7 Diversity Advantaging

17 Transgenerational Bridging

6 HR Process Re-Engineering

18 Strategic Sustainability In-Casting

19 A–Z Resilience

9 Trust Portfolio Management

20 Health, Hope & Happiness Empowerment

22 HR Hacktivism

8 HR Predictive Analytics

21 Onlife Performance Management

SME constellation

There are various definitions of SMEs which differ from country to country. In Switzerland a number of employees below 250 is what defines an SME.[255] However, it is recognized that in addition to enterprise size, the field of industry, the enterprises' scope of activity, the age of the enterprise, the owner's personal as well as other characteristic features all influence the operations of SMEs and, within it, SMEs' HR resource use and management.[256]

More than just definitions, it is key to understanding that SMEs make up over 99% of commercial companies in Switzerland and create two-thirds of the jobs in the country.[257] SMEs are also very important in other European countries, making up for 70–80% of European enterprises, thus signaling the global economic weight of such businesses.[258]

It seems logical that SMEs enjoy a greater ability to make rapid organizational and strategic changes due to their small size, which will be increasingly relevant and essential in a VUCA[259] world, yet SMEs naturally possess fewer HR technical skills and have less time than larger firms.[260] That is why for some SMEs the issues of HR practices still focus on survivability, reducing its scope to the mere administration of employees – and thus implicitly giving HR a non-strategic role rather than the mission to achieve competitive advantages and alignment. However, and despite the evident constraints, it is clear that ideally SMEs should not ignore the importance of their people or that they ought to continuously improve their HR management.[261] It is then paramount to identify the human and financial resources that need to be mobilized to run a successful HR activity in an SME.

Interestingly, it appears that most HR activities can be outsourced. While specific activities – which require considerable knowledge of the existing human capital and the organization structure, processes and culture – may be best handled internally, the trend to outsource HR services to outside labor market intermediaries is increasing.[262] We will see a growing number of startups and SMEs tackle these emerging markets in the outliers Disciplines.

With the following SME constellation, we propose to delimit an HR upgrade to activities that are paramount for future success and not easily outsourceable.

255 Swiss SME Portal. (2020). *Facts and figures on SMEs in Switzerland*. Retrieved from https://www.kmu.admin.ch/kmu/en/home/facts-and-trends/facts-and-figures.html.
256 Csillag, S., Csizmadia, P., Hidegh, A. L. & Szászvári, K. Á. (2019). Typical features of family-owned SME's HR practices. *Prosperitas*, v(1), 54–75,140.
257 Swiss SME Portal. (2020). *Facts and trends*. Retrieved from https://www.kmu.admin.ch/kmu/en/home/fakten-und-trends.html.
258 Mandl, I. (2008). Overview of family business relevant issues. Austrian Institute for SME Research in Co-operation with WVO-EHSL Brussels and Turku School of Economics, p.2.
259 Volatile, Uncertain, Complex, and Ambiguous.
260 Swiss SME Portal.(2020). *Necessary resources for digital transformation*. Retrieved from https://www.kmu.admin.ch/kmu/en/home/fakten-und-trends/digitalisierung/notwendige-ressourcen-fuer-die-digitale-wende.html.
261 Csillag, S., Csizmadia, P. Hidegh, A.L. & Szaszvari, K. (2019). Typical features of *family-owned SME's HR practices*.
262 Wallo, A. & Kock, H. (2018). HR outsourcing in small and medium-sized enterprises. *Personnel Review, 47*(5), 1003–1018.

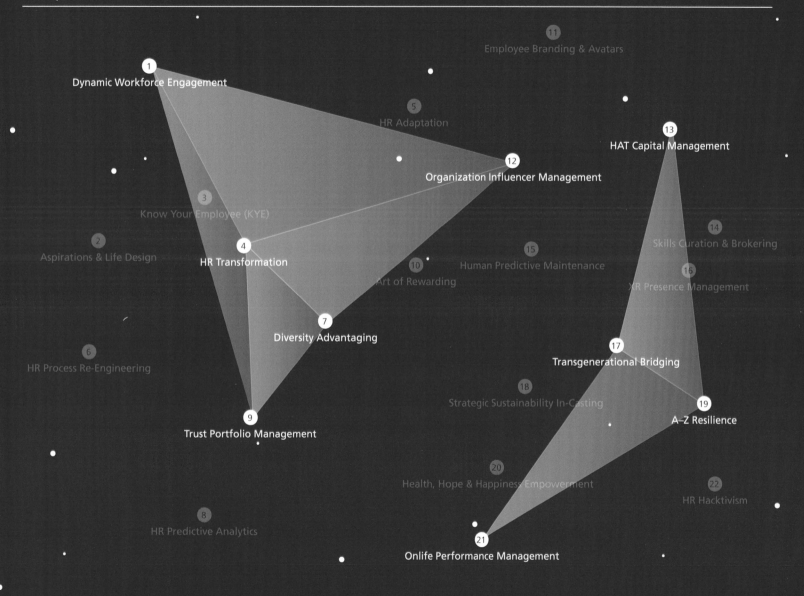

1 Dynamic Workforce Engagement

2 Aspirations & Life Design

3 Know Your Employee (KYE)

4 HR Transformation

5 HR Adaptation

6 HR Process Re-Engineering

7 Diversity Advantaging

8 HR Predictive Analytics

9 Trust Portfolio Management

10 Art of Rewarding

11 Employee Branding & Avatars

12 Organization Influencer Management

13 HAT Capital Management

14 Skills Curation & Brokering

15 Human Predictive Maintenance

16 XR Presence Management

17 Transgenerational Bridging

18 Strategic Sustainability In-Casting

19 A–Z Resilience

20 Health, Hope & Happiness Empowerment

21 Onlife Performance Management

22 HR Hacktivism

Public administration constellation

Managing in the public sector is widely different from managing in the world of business. The public sector operates by different rules, for different missions and within a much more regulated environment. Public administration can be a highly visible environment where metrics by which employees' performance is assessed are often very different than those used in for-profit organizations, because a good number of missions of public administrations are linked with fundamental societal needs, such as health, security, or education, which are hard to quantify. Failing to achieve the objective can have major negative consequences. This is thus even more important for managers in the public sector to empower, engage and motivate their workforce. Yet, despite offering employees to work for a greater purpose, managers in public administration are faced with significant challenges[263]:

- There is a prevailing negative attitude about civil servants, often seen as "overpaid and underemployed bureaucrats", which often reduces general workforce engagement.
- Public sector employees are often faced with frequent and abrupt changes of leadership, as many governments, municipalities or public agencies are led by elected individuals for a definite period of time. Moreover, some are politically appointed thus having specific policy agendas and are driven by short-term perspectives. To compensate, HR managers must put in place a very stable management team, capable of managing upwards and downwards as well as disseminating the institution's culture and values as widely as possible.
- Besides, when Management by Objective is still widely used, it is hard to implement in organizations which goals and missions are often hard to translate into objectively measurable units. HR leaders must focus even more on the institution's values, missions and global impact to generate employees' engagement and to drive its management.
- Although salaries in the public domain are often not as high as in the private sector, civil servants usually enjoy greater union protection and job security. As a result, once installed, and knowing that they can hardly be dismissed, some employees decrease their performance and become difficult to motivate. Recruitment therefore becomes a particularly crucial role.
- Conversely it is just as difficult to reward good employees for their engagement and hard work, as efficient incentive tools like bonuses, raises, stock options or benefits are often very limited. Managers need to be particularly resourceful in recognizing the loyalty of their employees.

There is no such thing as "public money", it is "taxpayers' money". Therefore, public administrations have a strong duty towards the taxpayers to manage their assets in the most efficient way, be they financial or human, which is why HR management gained traction[264] over the last decade.

Considering the specificities of the management of human capital in public administrations, the imposed transparency, and the expected reporting, the Public Administration constellation has its own form and upgrading priorities, as described hereafter.

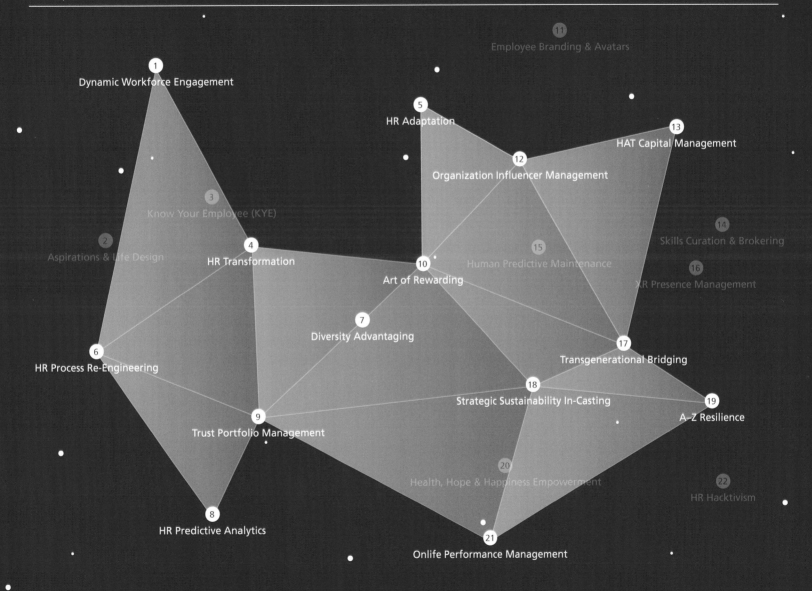

1. Dynamic Workforce Engagement
2. Aspirations & Life Design
3. Know Your Employee (KYE)
4. HR Transformation
5. HR Adaptation
6. HR Process Re-Engineering
7. Diversity Advantaging
8. HR Predictive Analytics
9. Trust Portfolio Management
10. Art of Rewarding
11. Employee Branding & Avatars
12. Organization Influencer Management
13. HAT Capital Management
14. Skills Curation & Brokering
15. Human Predictive Maintenance
16. XR Presence Management
17. Transgenerational Bridging
18. Strategic Sustainability In-Casting
19. A–Z Resilience
20. Health, Hope & Happiness Empowerment
21. Onlife Performance Management
22. HR Hacktivism

Multinationals constellation

While the practice of HR Management in multinational companies may be less defined and constrained by limited resources in finances and skills (as with SMEs) or face fewer challenges linked to rigid decision-making structure and legal constraints (as with PA), multinationals are faced with the challenges of globalization, multiculturalism and a multilingual workforce. HR leaders in multinationals must learn to navigate a complex world of national and international mores, cultures and laws. At the same time, multinationals generally enjoy greater human and financial resources which allow them to internalize more HR disciplines than SMEs or PAs. Therefore, HR leaders of multinationals carry greater strategic account-ability, and the challenges of facing and solving the constant evolutions of the workforce and rising skills obsolescence will increasingly be on their shoulders. Besides, enjoying greater means and visibility, they will also be perceived as trailblazers in the world of HR. It is even more important that they stay ahead of their time and pave the right way towards sustainable and positive futures.

Just as for SMEs, running a successful HR department is not merely about building a competitive advantage, it is about survival. Multinationals, unlike other types of organizations, are faced with particular challenges[265]:

- Multinationals typically manage a globalized and scattered workforce and encounter complex legal and ethical issues when conducting business across boarders. HR is responsible for keeping companies compliant with employment-related laws and tax codes and for the alignment across diverse languages, cultures and customs – and educational levels.
- When organizations are becoming more complex, distributed, robotized or hybrid, only a very diverse workforce can cover its specificities and achieve a 360-degree perspective. Successfully managing diversity makes it easier to deal with adversity,
- When globalization and multinational business has often meant salary dumping, organizations can hamper a bad reputation by communicating their sustainable approach to outsourcing which incorporates social responsibility rather than simply exploiting workers in poor countries.
- The trajectories of large organizations such as multinationals are very difficult to steer from when they are committed to a chosen strategic path. As a result, they must anticipate and plan for major changes well in advance so that they can reorient their human capital strategies in a timely manner.

263 Lavigna, R. (2014). Why government workers are harder to motivate. *Harvard Business Review*.
264 Boselie, P., Van Harten, J. & Veld, M. (2019). A human resource management review on public management and public administration research: Stop right there... before we go any further... *Public Management Review*, 23(4), 483–500.
265 Bolden-Barrett, V. (2017) What challenges do multinational firms face in the HR department? *Bizfluent*.

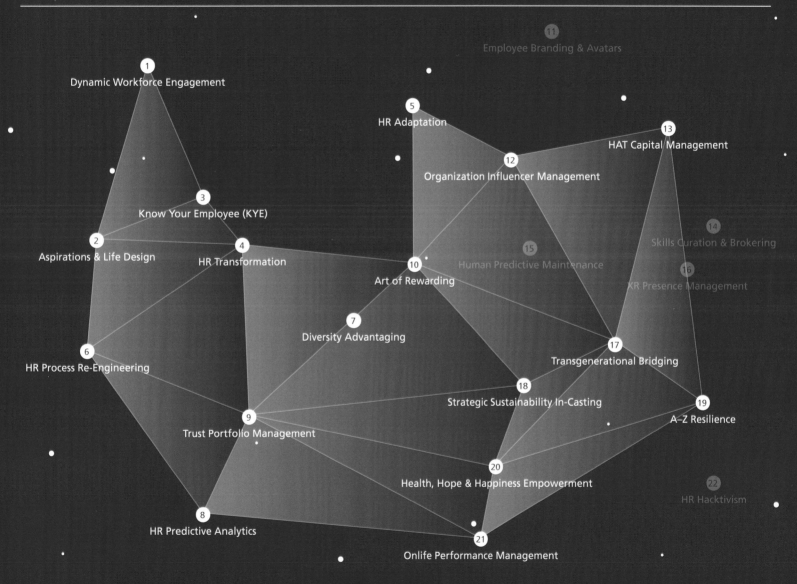

Dynamic Workforce Engagement

1

3 Know Your Employee (KYE)

2 Aspirations & Life Design

4 HR Transformation

5 HR Adaptation

11 Employee Branding & Avatars

13 HAT Capital Management

12 Organization Influencer Management

14 Skills Curation & Brokering

15 Human Predictive Maintenance

10 Art of Rewarding

16 XR Presence Management

7 Diversity Advantaging

6 HR Process Re-Engineering

17 Transgenerational Bridging

18 Strategic Sustainability In-Casting

19 A–Z Resilience

9 Trust Portfolio Management

20 Health, Hope & Happiness Empowerment

22 HR Hacktivism

8 HR Predictive Analytics

21 Onlife Performance Management

FOR STRATEGIES

Your workforce is your most valuable asset. The knowledge and skills they have represent the fuel that drives the engine of business, and you can leverage that knowledge.

Harvey Mackay, businessman and author

While the HR function is still often primarily seen as a resource center that delivers services ranging from recruitment to compensation and benefits, or dealing with legal employment contracts, it is increasingly put in the spotlight as the workforce orchestrator, aligning skills and work processes and organization with the company's strategic agenda.

As such, it should structure its growth and set its priorities according to the company's current main focus.

Instead of going all out and developing internal capabilities, choosing selected ones at random, following the HR Leader's preferences, or building up all 22 new Disciplines at once, organizations need to strategically upgrade and help build systemic readiness in line with the current leader's strategic agenda, exploiting the skills and mindset already available in-house.

It is clear that organizations do not and should not ground and establish their global strategy purely on the basis of some externally driven claim – think of data-driven, human-driven or environment-driven. This is even truer for their HR strategy. However, it is as well established that these three externally-driven examples are meta-strategies that clearly require a different type of skills and need to be tackled through synergies within the organization.

A technology and data-driven strategy embraces the use of data in decision-making, breaking down silos and enabling everyone across the organization to extract more value for its business from the data the organization already has. An organization can embrace a data-driven strategy if it is data-centric. In data-centric organizations, also called *algorithmic organizations* by Gartner, data belongs to everyone in the organization. It is an organizational asset. A data-centric organization is aware of that, declares data an asset, and protects it as such. It recognizes its value, and though it might not have a place on the balance sheet, it has an evident presence throughout the organization. When the whole organization has a vested interest in data, it ensures that the raw data is richer. As a result, the insights garnered are superior, they address the business problems (which have also been more accurately defined) more precisely and more importantly, the insights are understood better by those who make the decisions.

If the organization already has data-analysts, data-translators, and digitalization experts within its ranks, it makes full sense to start upgrading HR towards 2030 starting with data-driven disciplines.

By building data into every niche of the business and elaborating a data strategy, these organizations are laying the foundations for decreased operational costs and higher profits. All information, good and bad, important and not-so-important, has to be shared and made available to everyone. Available data is valuable, but finding or creating new data can be even more valuable. Data is collected and harvested from everywhere: internal, external, and paid data. Once the business problem is defined, the data needed to solve the problem is imagined, and then ways are devised to find it, if not already available. Data for which no known use currently exists is also retained, because of the possibility of it having value at some point in the future. Everyone can then have a holistic view of the data they need, and transparency and collaboration at all levels can be achieved while celebrating data successes to promote further a robust data sharing culture. Data-centric organizations will be able to leverage on this exquisitely cyberspatial asset, to exponentiate their operations. Although it may have stemmed from IT, data-driven culture has reached the arcane of marketing, finance, sales and now increasingly HR. If the organization already has data-analysts, data-translators, and digitalization experts within its ranks, it makes full sense to start upgrading HR towards 2030 starting with data-driven disciplines.

A particularly human and society-powered strategy and culture can be driven by the very mission of an organization that puts diversity, cohesion or inclusiveness at the core of its purpose. For companies in this specific configuration, it seems relevant to build on the available drive and passion shared by leaders and employees and initiate HR developments towards 2030 with HR disciplines strongly linked with the human dimension of business.

Environment and sustainability focused strategy and regenerative management practices are growing rapidly among the ranks of leaders. On the roadmap towards a more environmentally friendly business, it is coherent to focus on specific HR disciplines as an accelerating factor towards a greener future.

1 TECHNOLOGY & DATA-DRIVEN STRATEGY

- **1** Dynamic Workforce Engagement
- **3** Know Your Employee (KYE)
- **4** HR Transformation
- **5** HR Adaptation
- **6** HR Process Re-Engineering
- **8** HR Predictive Analytics
- **13** HAT Capital Management
- **15** Human Predictive Maintenance
- **16** XR Presence Management
- **22** HR Hacktivism

2 HUMAN & SOCIETY-POWERED STRATEGY

- **1** Dynamic Workforce Engagement
- **2** Aspirations & Life Design
- **3** Know Your Employee (KYE)
- **7** Diversity Advantaging
- **9** Trust Portfolio Management
- **10** Art of Rewarding
- **11** Employee Branding & Avatars
- **12** Organization Influencer Management
- **13** HAT Capital Management
- **14** Skills Curation & Brokering
- **17** Transgenerational Bridging
- **19** A–Z Resilience
- **20** Health, Hope & Happiness Empowerment
- **21** Onlife Performance Management
- **22** HR Hacktivism

3 ENVIRONMENT & SUSTAINABILITY FOCUSED STRATEGY

- **4** HR Transformation
- **7** Diversity Advantaging
- **15** Human Predictive Maintenance
- **18** Strategic Sustainability In-Casting
- **19** A–Z Resilience

HR LEADER 2030

A leader is a dealer in hope.

Napoleon Bonaparte (1769–1821)

HR Leader 2030

In this disrupted universe of work, the HR function will have to compose with some radically new disciplines. A different version of HR leaders is required to help organizations enter and thrive in and beyond the Fourth Industrial Revolution.

HR leaders are under more scrutiny than ever to act and anticipate as their role suddenly takes on a higher strategic importance for both the managing boards and the workforce. Indeed, Chief HR Officers (CHROs) are at the fulcrum of organizations' response to the COVID-19 crisis just as Chief Financial Officers (CFOs) were during the global financial crisis. With the acceleration of digitalization due to COVID-19, HR has been on the front line to help organizations evolve, and for some of them, to finally bring them into the era of the Fourth Industrial Revolution. Guiding organizations into the future has just started.

As change will prevail and increase in the years to come, HR leaders have a unique opportunity to up their game to deliver real added value in today's business setting. "HR needs to stop asking for a seat at the table. Instead, create a new table: Figure out how the organization can channel human energy to create value".[267] This means that HR professionals need to rethink their own pertinence and develop new capabilities that will help them thrive and guide their organization through those changing times. In the upcoming era of constant and lifelong learning, HR leaders will be in charge of organizing and building the capabilities of the organization's workforce, starting with building up their own function's capabilities.

HR leaders will have to develop and master specific skills linked to communication and leadership:

267 Bolles, G. A. (2020). LinkedIn post. Retrieved from https://www.linkedin.
    com/posts/gbolles_the-evolution-of-hr-an-uprisor-conversation-activi-
    ty-6672364620281352192-lsZy/.

 HARD AND FUNCTIONAL SKILLS
Develop business knowledge and leverage technology

 SOFT AND FUSION SKILLS
Build, grow and radiate trust

 AMPLIFYING AND INSPIRATIONAL SKILLS
Set the example, respect and gain respect

 TRANSFORMATION AND EVOLUTION SKILLS
Lead culture and knowledge development

Develop

Develop business knowledge
and leverage technology for business.

Organizations' purpose is evolving. From mere shareholder benefits generators to drivers of global good, the meaning of business is shifting. HR leaders need to integrate, live and promote those changes to align their actions with their organization's purpose.

Regardless of their organization's positioning, culture or values, HR leaders must be knowledgeable in the science and art of traditional HR – ranging from organizational psychology, to recruitment, all the way to compensation and benefits, yet recognizing that the field is increasingly getting broader and diversified, encompassing decision-making science, data science or environmental science. Leadership relying on credibility and credibility building on the pertinent use of valid, unique and privileged information, HR leaders must first learn how to compose with flooding data flows and bring meaning and coherence to the wells of available knowledge.

Besides, "as technology exponents, HR professionals have to access, advocate, analyze and align technology for information, efficiency, and relationships".[268] HR leaders must integrate and leverage technology, understanding how it strengthens the organization – its image and brand (outside) and the network of its own social relations (within).

Sitting in a powerful pivotal role, HR leaders must know how to use their power to anticipate and create favorable and desirable futures for the organization and for the humans that compose it. Deep knowledge of current transformation trends, intellectual curiosity, vision, imagination and creative thinking and doing, will be key in helping shape desirable futures for the organization. They must not only know the business as it operates today but be able to take strong positions to strategically shape the business for future successes.

268 Ulrich, D. (2016). HR at a crossroads. *Asia Pacific Journal of Human Resources*, 54(2), 148–164.

HR leaders must integrate and leverage technology, understanding how it strengthens the organization – its image and brand and the network of its own social relations.

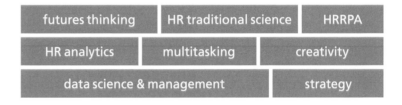

Build

Build, grow, and radiate trust
for engagement.

The adoption of intelligent technologies is putting pressure on organizations to build future-fit workforces capable of human–machine collaboration. HR leaders will increasingly need to identify, design and promote the value of individuals in a mixed workforce and to reassure employees with regards to the human-centric values of the organization. For employees to develop trust towards the organization and their executive representatives, such as HR leaders, they need to feel valued and aligned with the company culture. Concretely, effective HR professionals are perceived as credible activists when they build their personal trust by meeting commitments, building relationships, and growing in business acumen.[269] Only if they keep accessing and developing the right information, delivering tangible results, and sharing their mission broadly and in a compelling manner will they become trustworthy and be able to generate employee engagement.

In a post-factual era and paradoxically in an increasing transparency setting, HR leaders will need to tell the difference between the right and the wrong, between the important and the meaningless, and be able to communicate accordingly. Intellectual self-defense will be necessary.

Strategic reflections on global workforce trends or technology shifts will need to be translated into compelling narratives, concrete actions and tangible results for both the employees and the executive board. From concepts to projects, from ideas to results, pragmatism and action will be necessary to onboard employees on this change journey.

Regardless of the means or the style used, communication is only considered communication when the right message has come across. To become an effective communicator and to influence others in a positive way, HR leaders will need clear, consistent, and high-impact and multi-channel communications.

269 Ulrich, D. (2012). Exclusive: The six competencies to inspire HR professionals for 2012. *HR Magazine*.

Strategic reflections on global workforce trends or technology shifts will need to be translated into compelling narratives, concrete actions and tangible results for both the employees and the executive board.

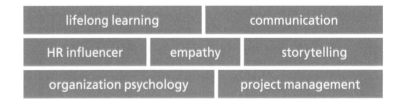

Set

Set the example, respect, and gain respect for efficient leadership.

A genuine people-centric attitude coupled with advanced people analytics will promote understanding of the workforce characteristics and a more situational leadership. If leadership is about showing the way and bringing people together to walk in the same direction towards the same goal, the HR Leader will have to lead from above, but first and foremost from within, connecting and engaging with their boards, peers and general workforce. Respected professionals lead from above and from within.

The traditional approach to strategy requires precise predictions and thus often leads executives to underestimate uncertainty, which can be downright dangerous. Yet, we have entered an era of rowing uncertainty, and efficient leaders need to apply new rules. If we can classify the levels of uncertainty surrounding strategic decision, from "clear enough future" to identified "alternative futures" up to "range of futures" or "true uncertainty",[270] the year 2020 has clearly proven that we are nearing level four: true uncertainty.

Respected professionals lead
from above and from within.

Strong leadership is needed in such times and it is hard. Leaders will have to manage diverse people, evolving dynamics, moving priorities, and radical changes. When the milestones for achieving strategic objectives disappear and inflection points arise on the planed trajectory to success, leaders are left with a mere compass indicating their great north and a vision to bring people together, inspire them and mobilize them. In the same way that a pilot communicates with his crew and passengers when encountering turbulence, HR leaders will need to take care of themselves (work–life balance), communicate constantly (physically and digitally), check with people on a personal level (empathy), be flexible, be nimble (agile), and first and foremost be real.[271]

270 Courtney, H. G., Kirkland, J. & Viguerie, S. P. (2000) Strategy under uncertainty. *McKinsey Quarterly*.
271 Robbins, M. (2020). Leading in the midst of uncertainty. *Forbes*.

work–life balance	diversity
decision-making	resilience
inclusivity	(digital) leadership

Lead

Lead culture and knowledge
development for sustained change.

A profound understanding of the Traits of Futures and clear
insight with regards to their impact on the Future of Work
and on organizational processes are key when driving an entity
and its workforce through the tumults of this ocean of changes.
HR leaders have long ceased to be mere human experts.
Today more than ever, they need to be strategists and generalists able to quickly get the big picture and skilled to grasp
implications from weak signals. Leaders "older than 45 years
who won't have an under 30-year-old mentor – not a mentee,
mentor – are going to miss fundamental shifts in thinking
that are happening",[272] HR leaders will thus have to organize
transgenerational networks.

In particular, HR leaders will need to integrate what drives
the current workforce and the emerging workforce, such as
the *New Value Schemes* and adapt narratives and actions

around it. Moreover, they will need to reorganize processes
around adapted praxes, needs and aspirations, such as remuneration methods, communication style and media, and operating
tools, as presented in the 22 Disciplines.

HR leaders must master the processes of individual and institutional change. To lead all traditional functions of HR and
develop the new disciplines proposed here, HR leaders must
orchestrate knowledge development and deployment, must
develop typical Swiss army knife capabilities, and must be
multifaceted and multi-tasking and -acting, available, and a
trusted companion.

272 Mentorloop (2019). *Having an under-30 mentor is the new shadowing
at work*. Retrieved from https://mentorloop.com/blog/under-30-mentor-
shadowing-at-work/.

HR leaders have long ceased to be mere human experts.
Today more than ever, they need to be strategists and
generalists able to quickly get the big picture and skilled
to grasp implications from weak signals.

(reverse) mentoring		CSR/SDG
holacracy	psychology	coaching
change management		foresight

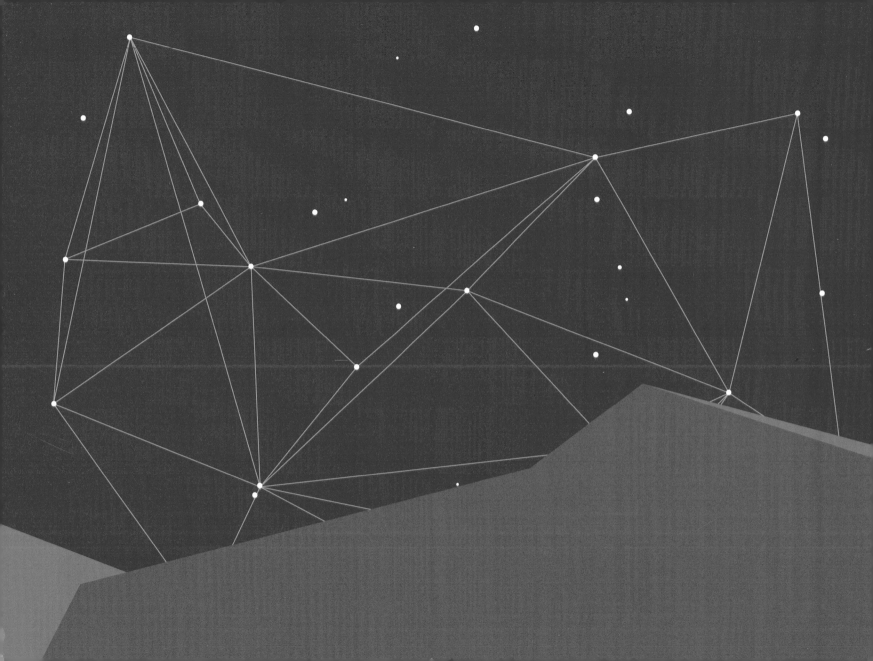

HR LEADER 2030

| futures thinking | HR trad. science | HRRPA | lifelong learning | communication | work–life balance | change mgmt | diversity | coaching |

| HR analytics | multitasking | creativity | HR influencer | empathy | storytelling | inclusivity | foresight | resilience | holacracy | CSR/SDG |

| data science & mgmt | strategy | organization psychology | project mgmt | decision-making | (digital) leadership | (reverse) mentoring |

AFTERWORD

Conclusions
and way forward

**WHAT DID WE SET OUT TO REACH,
AND WHAT DID WE ACHIEVE HERE?**

We wanted to write a book with a long-term, 10-year outlook to help leaders – from the HR world and beyond – prepare for the future. A future that is coming at us at an unexpected speed and which will bring along significant shifts.

As we have seen with the sudden COVID-19 disruptions on the world of work, it has become increasingly clear that learning today's theories to face and solve tomorrow's challenges is less and less useful. That is why we wrote this volume: a book ready for prime time in Academia and at the University, backed up by evidence-based trends and signals, and offering pragmatic development pathways towards 2030. We authored it having in mind both forward-looking scholars and present-oriented, pragmatic industry captains and HR directors, compelled to find answers for their inevitably obsolescing, fragmentarily morphing workforce. Our ambition is to leave them with more tools to navigate uncertainty, understand its consequences, and bring their organization to success.

MAKE SENSE OF THE NEW
We trust that by offering a chance to relate to the archetype suiting the most, the mythology is an atlas to help the reader situate in the evolving geography of the HR function and navigate its changes without winding up in uncharted waters.

UNDERSTAND THE FORCES IN PLACE

"The" future does not exist: there are multiple possible trajectories from today to 2030, and thus the future comes in many guises, what futurists call "images of the futures." These Traits of Futures have a connection to weak signals surfacing in the present, making them relatable and forward-looking at the same time, to provide a strong drive to long-term thinking for the futures of work and HR.

PREPARE A PATHWAY TOWARDS THE 22ND CENTURY

The Traits of Futures are the main forces to be factored in the equation of the futures. They model, like incorporeal potters, the clay describing the future landscape. Depending on their combination, the resulting "vase" has a different form, fit, and function. In this book we identify 22 of these "vases," the Disciplines, some evolving as bifurcation and recombination of existing HR roles today under the drive of the Traits, others blossoming in the fertile terrain of the futures.

UPSKILL YOURSELF

As new Disciplines will surface, aggregate and develop in the totipotent waters of the futures, new HR leaders will need to grow their skills to understand this sea, navigate its waves of change, and make the team thrive in a stable ship. HR leaders will have to keep developing hard and functional traditional HR skills and complement them with soft and fusion skills to build trust; amplify and deploy skills to gain respect through example; and develop transformation and evolution skills.

We acknowledge that change is never easy, and that the current and unprecedented uncertainty brings with it its important share of anxiety. Yet, we are being presented with extraordinary opportunities to shape our world towards positive futures.

Ideas shape our world, actions create it.
It is time to reclaim our right to hope.

Acknowledgements

The Authors wish to acknowledge the contributions of those whose dedicated work made the success of the HR Futures 2030 foresight workshop and its culmination in this book possible:

The Faculty of Business & Economics (HEC Lausanne) of the University of Lausanne (UNIL) and its leadership for allowing the creation of an entity focused entirely on the study of futures and for supporting and encouraging the HR Futures 2030 initiative.

The Dreamers & Designers of the content of this book, all key-actors within the world of HR and listed in the volume, for their involvement and their creativity during the workshop.

Mieke van de Capelle, CHRO of Firmenich, for her support both financial and in kind, and for sharing her own invaluable expertise in the field of HR.

HR Vaud, and its leadership, in particular **Jérôme Rudaz** and **Guy Zehnder**, for supporting this project both financially and in giving us access to their broad network of HR professionals.

Emmanuel Sylvestre, **Jeff van de Poël** and **Elodie Jantet** from the CSE – Centre de soutien à l'enseignement (Education Support Center) of the University of Lausanne for their support, enthusiasm, and passion in being part of the event. And thanks for all the great work with the visuals!

Quentin Ladetto, Foresight & Research Director at armasuisse S+T, for his enthusiasm, precious support and the very insightful discussions.

Mahwesh Khan and **Ben Thancanamootoo** for their support in facilitating the workshop.

Julien Savioz, our graphic designer, who gave shape and materiality to our ideas with great creativity, giving our book a unique visual identity.

Muriel Rubin, as the orchestrator of this initiative at the Futures Lab of the Faculty of Business & Economics (HEC Lausanne) at the University of Lausanne (UNIL), for her priceless human skills and for the essential technical, organizational and project manage-ment prowess she provided for making the HR Futures 2030 workshop possible. We also thank her for her nitpicking attention to detail in co-copy-editing the manuscript of this volume.

Our publishing team at Routledge, that patiently dealt with our impossible timelines and incredibly compressed schedules to create this book. **Amy Laurens** and **Alex Atkinson** were the top support and the finest Editors we could possibly have wished for, as well as **Cathy Hurren** and **Lorraine Savage** – our Production Editor and proofreader – who with their remarkable passion for details pushed us to be the best authors we can be.

We also want to thank each other. We love the future – we are going to spend the rest of our lives there. We have learnt beyond our expectations in this rich, intense, and sometimes rocky journey taking us to write this volume. In an unprece-dented world situation characterized by the pandemic and a lockdown, we lived dematerialization through and through, creating our cyber-physical collaborative space from zero. We have made the most of our differences and our complemen-tarities and constantly worked at building on each other's strengths and creative, even crazy, ideas.

The future is shaped by our imagination…
So why create a boring one?

About
the authors

ISABELLE CHAPPUIS

lic. oec. HSG, is an economist by training and an expert in continuing education. She is passionate about the Future of Work and the place of humans within it.

After her Master's degree in marketing and human resources from the University of St. Gallen in Switzerland, and a few years working in finance and reinsurance in Zurich, she has held leading positions in executive education at the University of Lausanne for 15 years. She has been Director of the Executive MBA program of at HEC Lausanne, the Faculty of Business & Economics of the University of Lausanne (UNIL), and then founder and Director of the Executive Education entity of the Faculty, before she moved on to the Future.

Isabelle bet on her curiosity and competence about the Future of Work, the Future of Skills and the many challenges and opportunities lying ahead. She founded and is now the Director of the Futures Lab, the foresight unit of HEC Lausanne, bringing foresight and education together to help humans take back ownership of their future.

Isabelle Chappuis is fluent in French, German, and English. In 2020 she was elected to the *Forum des 100*, the group of the 100 personalities who shape the French-speaking part of Switzerland.

Ms Chappuis regularly gives keynotes on the Future of Work and Positive Futures. She genuinely cares about people, transitions, and accelerating their success.

DR. GABRIELE RIZZO
Ph.D., APF, is a visionary futurist and an enthusiastic innovator.

A Ph.D. in String Theory and Astrophysics grown into a Defense leading expert in foresight, he is the NATO's Member at Large ("world-class expert drawn from academia, industry or government from the Nations") in Strategic Foresight and Futures Studies, and the former advisor to the Italian Minister of Defense for Futures. Dr. Rizzo serves as Board member both for policy strategy (in EU organizations surpassing $2B worth and scoring with honors on EU reviews) and for scientific research (leading the world's largest community of 5000+ Defense scientists).

Gabriele advises Governments and Defenses on long-term strategies, foresight, game-changing technologies, and innovation convergence. The U.S., UK, Italy, Switzerland, NATO, United Nations, European Defense Agency, and other allied Governments and Fortune Global500 companies all number him among their ranks. He has been leading deep futures vision in the 2060 timeframe of the U.S. Space Force, the U.S. Air Force, the U.S. Air Force Research Laboratories, the Italian Prime Minister's Grand Strategy 2040, and several other senior major engagements on strategic foresight and futures. His works inform $1 trillion worth of Defense planning. Some were evaluated "important pillars of strategy and implementation of R&I" by the EU. Others shape industrial investments in Research, Development, and Innovation for more than $20B in 2020.

Dr. Rizzo routinely gives keynotes in the U.S. and Europe, and is passionate about complexity, singularity, and peace.